Developing
Successful
K–8 Schools

This book is dedicated my wife, Michele Wiles.

Developing **Successful** K–8 Schools

A Principal's Guide

Jon Wiles

CORWIN
A SAGE Company

For information:

Corwin
A SAGE Company
2455 Teller Road
Thousand Oaks, California 91320
(800) 233-9936
Fax: (800) 417-2466
www.corwinpress.com

SAGE Ltd.
1 Oliver's Yard
55 City Road
London EC1Y 1SP
United Kingdom

SAGE Pvt. Ltd.
B 1/I 1 Mohan Cooperative
    Industrial Area
Mathura Road, New Delhi 110 044
India

SAGE Asia-Pacific Pte. Ltd.
33 Pekin Street #02-01
Far East Square
Singapore 048763

Printed in the United States of America.

Library of Congress Cataloging-in-Publication Data

Wiles, Jon.
Developing successful K-8 schools : a principal's guide / Jon Wiles.
    p. cm.
Includes bibliographical references and index.
ISBN 978-1-4129-6616-0 (cloth)
ISBN 978-1-4129-6617-7 (pbk.)
   1. Elementary school principals—United States. 2. Middle school principals—United States. I. Title.

LB2831.92.W53 2009
371.12'012—dc22

2009006444

This book is printed on acid-free paper.

09   10   11   12   13   10 9 8 7 6 5 4 3 2 1

Acquisitions Editor:	Debra Stollenwerk
Associate Editor:	Julie McNall
Production Editor:	Veronica Stapleton
Copy Editor:	Ed Meidenbauer
Typesetter:	C&M Digitals (P) Ltd.
Proofreader:	Susan Schon
Cover Designer:	Karine Hovsepian

Contents

Preface

For the third time in a century, the upper grades of the elementary school are being retooled. In 1909, the first junior high school appeared. In 1965, the junior high school was replaced by the American middle school. And, now, the new K–8 school is emerging in cities, the suburbs, and the countryside schools of the United States. The transition to the K–8 model, which is just starting, represents a major change in the way we educate our young people. It is particularly interesting that this movement has begun without legislation, significant discussion, or even much media fanfare.

Most educators know that this isn't the first time we have tried the eight-grade elementary school. Before the turn of the 20th century, virtually all elementary schools included grades 1–8. In fact, four out of five students who had graduated high school before 1920 had attended a K–8 school. Those schools were abandoned during the 20th century, for a variety of reasons, but now they're back. What is causing this return to yesteryear?

There are many forces working to reintroduce the eight-year-plus-kindergarten school (K–8) to our educational system. First and foremost is the fact that there is strong research evidence that leaving students in an elementary school through the eighth grade results in better standardized test scores (see Resource A). Also, it is clear that parents want a smaller neighborhood elementary school where their child is close by and known by teachers. Finally, there seem to be fewer problems with truancy, discipline referrals, suspensions, and student attitudes in K–8 schools. In fact, there are a surprisingly large number of reasons why the new K–8 school makes good common sense.

Unfortunately, the good news about K–8 education seems to stop there. Many new K–8 schools, like middle schools before them, are being created for the wrong reasons. Some districts have too many facilities and want to consolidate their small schools. Some districts are looking for a way to lower the high school dropout problem by cutting out one student transition between schools. Still other districts are willing to try the K–8 model to increase student performance on state tests of educational standards. Finally, some schools and districts are just getting on the K–8 bandwagon. All of these constitute a less-than-adequate reason for making this change.

Overall, there doesn't seem to be a sound curriculum prescription available for developing a new K–8 program in many schools, whether they are of the conversion variety or a brand-new program. Unless the question of mission is addressed, now, the K–8 school is bound to experience the same decline in the future as did the junior high school and the middle school. This book, *Developing Successful K–8 Schools*, seeks to fill that void by offering experienced guidance and suggestions to communities developing these new programs.

On the face of it, existing elementary schools and middle schools can be combined fairly easily because they share many of the same values. Both programs have a philosophy focusing on children's development. Both programs espouse "general education" instead of simple academic specialization. Both programs have teachers used to flexible organization and diverse methodologies to meet the individual differences of K–8 students.

But, despite these areas of agreement, there has always been an enormous problem with the role of subject matter in the intermediate grades. Both the junior high school and the middle school failed to clearly define the academic curriculum of the upper elementary grades, and the new K–8 model will certainly fail also unless it clearly defines this foundational program variable. Administrators who are leading their schools into the K–8 model must pay particular attention to the instructional design of the upper grades (Grades 5–8), an area referred to as an "educational wasteland" by some critics. There are many new ideas in this book about how the K–8 school should be structured. The author, a veteran educator of 30 years in elementary and intermediate schools, suggests a four-tier developmental curriculum model along the lines of human developmental stages. Content, in the form of state learning standards, can be used to define the "what" of the program. Skills for thinking and learning, universally prescribed for life in the 21st century, can constitute the common denominator for all students. Ten instructional methods, found in effective elementary and middle schools for meeting student needs, can help us implement the instructional program at the building level.

PURPOSE AND ORGANIZATION OF THE BOOK

The reader of this book will find all of the ingredients necessary for developing an exemplary K–8 program: everything from a rationale, curriculum design, instructional organization, planning steps, and assessment technique. In

Chapter 1, the author provides a historical context that explains and rationalizes the evolution of the K–8 school. In Chapter 2, the new K–8 program is connected to mandated state curriculum standards, showing how those standards can be more effectively applied in K–8 schools. Chapter 3 develops the notion of a seamless grade-to-grade K–8 program, one that will solve articulation problems and increase student achievement. Chapter 4 introduces a novel four-tier instructional program based on sound human development studies and designed to negate traditional academic issues. In Chapter 5, the author discusses the return-on-investment for parents, students, teachers, and administrators who support the K–8 school. Chapter 6 provides the reader with step-by-step processes (facilities, curriculum, instruction, resource uses, technology, and parent–community relations) for developing this program at the building level. Finally, in Chapter 7, the author outlines the assessment processes needed to guide and to validate the new K–8 school.

SPECIAL FEATURES DESIGNED TO HELP PRACTITIONERS IN THEIR WORK

Resources found at the conclusion of this book include a comprehensive research survey of K–8 programs (Resource A), content standards organizations (Resource B), sample designs for using the Internet in K–8 classrooms (Resource C), a full glossary of terms relating to K–8 education for community members (Resource D), K–8 instructional resources for implementing the K–8 program found on the Internet (Resource E), and suggested reading for those seeking further information about the new K–8 program (Resource F). This book also contains a variety of practical tools such as chapter summaries, questions for study groups, detailed references, and boxed summaries of important chapter features.

These prescriptions and resources are presented to the reader as a kind of tool kit for developing possible solutions to the problems and issues faced by educators at this level of education for over a century. Although there is no absolute formula for the new K–8 school, there are extensive and ready-to-use resources for developing the K–8 school. Using this book, *Developing Successful K–8 Schools*, each faculty and community can both set and activate priorities and preferred patterns in a new K–8 program for their students.

Acknowledgments

Corwin wishes to acknowledge the following peer reviewers for their editorial insight and guidance.

Dr. Rich Bauscher
Superintendent
Middleton School District
Middleton, Idaho

Dr. Elizabeth J. Lolli
Superintendent
Monroe Local Schools
Monroe, Ohio

Marie Blum
Superintendent
Canaseraga Central School District
Canaseraga, New York

Stephen Shepperd
Building Principal, Retired
Sunnyside Elementary School
Kellogg, Idaho

Robert A. Frick, EdD
Superintendent
Lampeter-Strasburg School District
Lampeter, Pennsylvania

Emily Shoemaker
Professor of Education
University of La Verne
La Verne, California

Jill Gildea, EdD
Superintendent
Harrison School District #36
Wonder Lake, Illinois

About the Author

Jon Wiles is a highly experienced educator who has provided curriculum leadership to schools and educational agencies for more than thirty years. His specialty is the creation and implementation of curriculum plans. Dr. Wiles's work as an educational consultant has taken him to hundreds of agencies in more than forty different states and to serve in a dozen foreign nations in Europe, Asia, Africa, and the Caribbean. Dr. Wiles is the author or coauthor of twelve widely used books addressing curriculum and educational leadership. His text *Curriculum Development: A Guide to Practice* (Seventh Edition) has been used for nearly thirty years in colleges and universities throughout the world to train curriculum leaders. Other areas of publication by Dr. Wiles include teacher training, administration, school supervision, theory of change, politics of education, middle-grades education, and technology. Dr. Wiles lives with his wife Michele on the northeast coast of Florida, and can be reached at J_MWiles@bellsouth.net.

Here Comes the New K–8 School

A new school organization is quietly emerging in the city systems, suburban communities, and rural districts of the United States. In most cases, the formation of the new K–8 school results from combining elementary and middle school programs. Approximately 5,000 of this nation's 45,000 elementary and middle schools have already converted to this new curriculum design, and dozens of additional schools are joining the movement each month. This new K–8 program promises to change the way America educates its children.

The attraction of the K–8 school model comes from many things: a promise of better testing achievement, greater parental choice, a perceived cost effectiveness, smaller and more personal learning environments, lowered secondary school dropout rates, and the ability to retain community support for our schools. It is largely a commonsense movement. This new emerging curriculum can be relatively seamless from kindergarten through the eighth grade and can be defined by state learning standards and 21st century thinking skills. The new K–8 movement is altering the curriculum in elementary and middle schools across America and will soon change the way teachers operate in the classroom of those schools.

ORIGINS OF THE NEW K–8 SCHOOL

To fully understand the meaning of this new and emerging educational design, it is useful to review what we know about traditional elementary and middle school programs in America. These programs share a historic commitment to child-centeredness and to the concept of general education in Grades K–8. Both today's K–5 elementary programs and the 6–8 middle school programs have a long history of successfully educating children and young adolescents in America. Yet there seems to be something wrong with the way in which these two traditional programs are functioning at the present and it is this dissatisfaction with the status quo that is driving the K–8 movement in the United States, community by community.

The modern K–5 elementary school has evolved during the past 200 years from a narrow curriculum devoted to teaching reading, writing, and arithmetic to a much broader program that encompasses not only learning skills but also a variety of learning experiences. Less than 25 years after the Pilgrims landed at Plymouth Rock (1620), the colonies were establishing schools, and these first elementary schools taught a kind of civic literacy curriculum. The basic assumption about educating children in those times was that they were like miniature adults and susceptible to evil forces (the Devil). Schools were seen as places where these "empty vessels" would be filled with useful knowledge and where, sometimes, it might be necessary to "beat the devil" out of children.

A new model of education for children began to form in the late 19th century based on humanistic (person-centered) ideas. Charles Darwin significantly influenced this new model with his theory of evolution; if plants and animals adapt to their environment, so also might children. Children were not empty containers to be filled, but rather dynamic organisms with many growth possibilities.

Three European educators also influenced the early elementary schools of America with their ideas. The French philosopher Jean-Jacques Rousseau contributed the notion that children were good, not bad; "noble savages" he called them. Johann Pestalozzi, a Swiss educator, encouraged schools to be holistic in their approach, teaching to the head, the heart, and the hand. The German Frederick Froebel, father of the kindergarten, wrote that children's learning should be built around the interests and experience of students. He saw learning as social interaction, experimentation, and trial interactions with the environment.

America's most famous educator, John Dewey, contributed to the philosophy and methodology of the elementary school in his work between 1884 and 1905. Dewey proposed a natural school, centered on the development of children, where a climate of positivism would prevail. Dewey held that subject matter was for living and should be integrated into everyday life experiences. Education was to be a dynamic process, with the student—rather than the teacher—being the primary player.

This new way of thinking about the elementary school became known as the *progressive* approach, as opposed to the traditional approach. Progressive education differed in many ways from the old way of educating (see Figure 1.1), especially in the way the teacher and students interacted. Because students in elementary schools were not simply small adults, and

Figure 1.1 Contrasting models for education 1900

Traditional Model	Progressive Model
Human nature is imperfect and must be "made." Children are incomplete adults.	Humans are good and their ultimate form results from interaction with their environment.
Students are to be controlled and corrected by the teachers.	Students grow naturally and only need guidance by teachers.
Common and structured learning is desirable.	Learning is always an individual experience.
A fixed and standardized curriculum is appropriate for children.	Curriculum should be individualized and developmentally appropriate.
Teachers have the knowledge and share it with students.	Teachers are also learners and should provide guidance to young learners.
Schools should be knowledge-based.	Schools should be based on learning experiences.

because they were all unique in their development, the organization and outcomes of learning had to be more flexible. These ideas about educating were strongly reinforced by early psychology in the United States and studies of human development (i.e., early childhood education, gifted education, exceptional education, and middle school education) throughout the 20th century.

The structure of the American elementary school in the late 19th century and early 20th century included Grades 1–8 in most states. The introduction of the Grades 7–9 junior high school in 1909 led many districts to restructure their elementary schools in a Grades 1–6 pattern. Junior high schools multiplied rapidly until the 1940s and then began to decline. Many junior highs soon became small models of the senior high school.

A major problem for the junior high school in the United States was the inclusion of the ninth grade. Because students in attendance had to earn high school credits in that grade, much instructional flexibility was lost. Also, the fully adolescent ninth grader in the junior high school did not seem to belong with the students experiencing the onset of puberty.

In the mid-1960s, the junior high school program, always modeled after the high school, began to be replaced by a hybrid institution called the *middle school*. The middle school originated as a restructured junior high and then took its modern shape in the 1960s to become America's most original curriculum design. At first, it was difficult to determine the difference between a junior high school and a middle school, but as the middle school became established, the differences became more pronounced (see Figure 1.2).

Figure 1.2   Contrasting junior highs and middle schools

Junior High School	Middle School
Housing Grades 7–9	Housing Grades 6–8
Based on high school model	More like extended elementary school
Content-based curriculum	Balanced curriculum features content, skills, and personal development
Fixed curriculum, few electives	Exploratory, rich, and flexible curriculum
Highly structured organization	Very flexible organization
Teachers as subject specialist	Teachers in interdisciplinary teams

Acknowledging the developmental difference between a child, a "preadolescent," and a full adolescent, the new middle school staked out the sixth, seventh, and eighth grades as the appropriate grade combinations for this middle group (The Berkeley Growth Studies and Harvard Growth Studies, 1962). This recombining of grades effectively left the existing elementary schools as a combination of Grades 1–5 or, after 1970, K–5.

Middle schools quickly developed a clear philosophy and mission. These schools were to be a special program of education for 10–14-year-old students who were experiencing a unique period of growth and development. These students would go through puberty and make the transition from older childhood to young adulthood under the middle school tutelage. The students would be characterized by their vast differences, and the school would have to be extremely flexible in its organization to accommodate this wide range of learners. A host of organizational structures became common to middle schools including block schedules, team teaching, interdisciplinary instruction, advisory guidance programs, exploratory wheels, and intramural programs.

Middle schools in the United States experienced phenomenal growth between 1970 and 1990, becoming the organizational format (Grades 6–8) for two-thirds of all intermediate students. The promise of being able to meet the needs of all pupils in attendance was seductive, and many middle schools did serve their students exceedingly well during this time period; others, did not.

By the early 1980s, middle school programs across America began to experience a series of fatal problems. Funding, following the Vietnam War, was a major difficulty for the complex and sophisticated middle school programs that needed substantial resources to operate. The legislative response to these financial difficulties, focusing and narrowing the curriculum by the use of performance standards, was the antithesis of middle school philosophy. Second, there was no effective evaluation to prove that middle schools worked better than junior high schools (Wiles, 1975). Finally, middle schools failed to define the content portion (subject matter) of the curriculum resulting in a tug-of-war by competing pressure groups about the purpose of intermediate education. By the early 1990s, warning signs were appearing that many middle schools were not working so well. This was particularly true in large urban middle schools and small rural middle schools.

From the mid-1990s until the present, there has been a growing voice from national commissions, educators, and parents calling for reform and another kind of lower school in America. The public is asking for a school relevant to the needs of the 21st century. Educators desire a more cost-effective and efficient school, one that can demonstrate academic results. Parents seem to want a more personal program, closer to home, where their children will be safe and known, and where it is certain that meaningful learning is taking place. This drive for restructuring elementary and intermediate programs by all these groups, growing daily, is the force behind the new American K–8 school emerging as the 21st century model program.

RATIONALE FOR CHANGING THE SCHOOL DESIGN

A substantial debate about what needs to be done with our schools has been going on for a decade in the literature of intermediate education in the United States. Involved in these discussions have been traditional elementary school educators, middle school educators, and some advocates for a new "elemiddle" or K–8 school. These groups have more in common than they have differences, and their philosophies of education are remarkably similar. The hundreds of articles written over the past 10 years about educating students in kindergarten through eighth grade have been more about *how* than *what*.

School districts in rural, suburban, and urban areas have entered into these on-going discussions, speaking loudly by their actions in establishing K–8 schools. At the time of this writing, more than 20 of the largest urban districts in America have committed to restructuring, employing the new K–8 configuration (see Figure 1.3). These local decisions to abandon middle schools or to add-on three grades to traditional elementary schools have not always been made for educational reasons. Nonetheless, the fact that so many K–8 schools are presently being created in urban systems and rural districts, and now many suburban districts, has significantly influenced the on-going professional discussion. Almost without rationale, planning, or funding, a major change is beginning to unfold in how Americans will educate their children.

The reasons given by school districts for restructuring into a K–8 pattern are many and varied. Some are restructuring because of failed middle school programs. Some districts, undoubtedly, are shifting student

Figure 1.3 Twenty-one large urban school districts restructured using the K–8 model

Baltimore	Memphis	Pittsburgh
Boston	Milwaukee	Rochester
Chicago	New Orleans	Salt Lake City
Cincinnati	New York	San Diego
Cleveland	Newark	San Francisco
Dayton	Oklahoma City	Trenton
Louisville	Philadelphia	Washington, DC

populations around to meet facility needs. Some districts are reacting to the costly dropout pattern in the early years of the high school. And, in some large urban districts, internal research is driving the K–8 transformation.

In those studies that compare student performances in K–8 schools with student performance in 6–8 middle schools, the K–8 students are found to do better on standardized achievement tests in all existing studies. Self-studies in districts also find that K–8 students attend school more often, have fewer discipline referrals, are suspended less frequently, and have better overall attitudes toward school. Many of these studies are not "causal," and most are lacking accepted research designs. These studies are summarized for the reader in Resource A at the end of this book.

The literature on the new K–8 school provides a long list of advantages for changing models. Twenty of the more common arguments are presented in Figure 1.4.

Looking at the many reasons for supporting K–8 education models, the reader will note major categories of thought. For example, parents favor a smaller neighborhood school where their children can attend uninterrupted for 9 years. Busing and an unnecessary transition to a middle school would be avoided. Siblings could attend the same school, thereby lessening the transportation burden for parents.

In such a school, teachers would know the students and the school would presume to be safer. Special needs of children would be known better by teachers. Discipline and suspensions would be less frequent. Students would be more mature and secure and would drop out of high school less often.

Administrators and teachers would favor a seamless K–8 curriculum that would result in better teaching and better student achievement. Students would not have to deal with a transition in the sixth grade and would have better attitudes at school. Older students could have leadership experiences in working with younger students at the school site.

Teachers, too, would be more secure and would turn over less often.

Figure 1.4 Twenty arguments for K–8 schools

1. Better academic achievement
2. Better student attitudes toward school
3. Safety in neighborhood schools
4. Fewer disciplinary problems
5. One less school transition for students
6. Teachers know kids for 9 years
7. Ease of transportation for parents with siblings in same school
8. Lower dropout rate in high school
9. Personal small-school identity
10. Technology allows in-depth academics and specialization
11. More attention to at-risk students
12. Lessens district busing requirements
13. Parents more comfortable with schools
14. Can run a middle school program inside the K–8 building
15. Continuous progress is more probable
16. Seamless curriculum with better articulation between the grades
17. Teachers more qualified for child-centered approach
18. Possible for students to experience more leadership roles
19. Less teacher turnover
20. Discipline and suspensions lowered

Persistent arguments about the need for more or less academic specialization in the upper grades could be met by remodeling schools- (cheaper than building) to provide special study areas, using new learning technologies to access in-depth knowledge, placing academic magnet schools within elementary schools, and even by running a traditional middle school program right inside the K–8 building.

These seemingly sound and convincing arguments favoring the K–8 school, however, have been challenged repeatedly in the literature, and in the field, by specific reservations about the curriculum found in K–8 schools (see Figure 1.5). There are genuine concerns, for example, about the academic nature of the upper grades in a K–8 school.

There can be little doubt that a substantial and genuine curriculum argument might be made against converting to K–8 schools. Preparation for high school requires in-depth work in academic disciplines, and most elementary teachers do not have much subject matter depth in their training. Due to the small size of most neighborhood K–8 schools (400–450 pupils), these schools may not have enough teachers to offer live, upper-level courses (algebra) or specialized courses (languages). In addition,

Figure 1.5 Reservations concerning K–8 schools

1. Fewer advanced academic courses (such as algebra) are available.
2. Major problems with redistricting for attendance may occur.
3. Science labs, music rooms, and special facilities are absent.
4. The possibility of student bullying increases.
5. Sexual maturation of older students creates social problems.
6. Sports programs and traditions decline.
7. Major certification problems exist for teachers in many states.
8. Libraries are superior and more grade-appropriate in middle schools.
9. "Dumbing down" the academic curriculum is a distinct possibility.

laboratories will not be available for lab sciences, the fine arts, and advanced music. Sports programs will necessarily be diluted. Libraries will, in most cases, be inadequate for in-depth study.

Planners of new K–8 schools will need to consider these reservations carefully. It is obvious to the author that there must be a focus on the curriculum in planning any new K–8 school and how such a school should be organized. This shift in the intermediate curricular program defines the purpose of this book.

BEDROCK BELIEFS ABOUT EDUCATING CHILDREN

As noted earlier, the various programs that serve students from kindergarten to eighth grade in the United States share the same core values and assumptions about human development and learning (see Figure 1.6). For over a century, elementary schools, junior high schools, and middle schools have seen child development (not subjects) as the organizer for the curriculum. The development of young children, older children, preadolescents, and adolescents, has been studied extensively, and there is wide acceptance of the idea that children develop in an orderly manner but at different rates. There are models of growth that are widely referenced by both elementary and middle school educators (Elkind, 1993; Gardner, 1983; Gessell, 1946; Havighurst, 1962; Piaget, 1969). Using these models, the educators have fashioned "developmentally appropriate" curriculums for learning.

Elementary and middle school educators see the child as a dynamic organism capable of considerable learning. These educators also share the belief that children learn by interacting with their environment. The lower school educators believe that previous experiences (prior learning) in life determines the readiness of the child to succeed in school. Student motivation to learn, they feel, is present when the school task and student interests overlap. Elementary and middle grades teachers generally agree that students should be the primary focus of any K–8 school program.

Figure 1.6   Bedrock beliefs of elementary and middle grades education

- The child is the focus of the curriculum.
- Human development is predictable and orderly.
- Knowledge, skills, and experiences are foundational.
- The program is broad, balanced, and "whole child."
- Learning should be developmentally appropriate.
- Subject matter should be integrated and applied to the real world.
- Students learn best in a positive climate.
- Prior experience determines readiness to learn.
- Relevance for the student activates motivation to learn.
- Families and community are partners in school learning.
- All students can learn.
- All students should experience success in school.

Planners for K–8 education must consider carefully any district or community preK programs that will establish the foundation for the new schools. PreK programs in the United States differ greatly in the degree to which they are social or academic in design. Certainly, a preK school undergirding the new K–8 program must provide students with experiences that will increase their awareness and understanding of what is to follow. Working backwards, K–8 school leaders should actively suggest appropriate learning tools and experiences to those operating the district preK programs. Such articulation is rarely found in public, private, and parochial schools.

The environment for learning in a K–8 school is believed to be very important at this level of education, and both the elementary and the middle school educator would promote a positive and supportive learning climate at all times. The family and the community, at this level of schooling, are perceived as important partners in the learning process. Where possible, these educators agree, learning should be integrated and applied to the real world of the student.

Finally, both elementary and middle grades educators would promote a broad, general, foundational program of learning. They feel there should be room for differences, expansion, and success in learning for all students. The "whole child" curriculum of the K–8 grades should be both expansive and exploratory.

The appropriateness of the K–8 curriculum model, versus the K–6 model, or the K–5, 6–8 combination, is not a question of *what* to teach but of *how* to teach. The relevance or appropriateness of the curriculum configuration will depend on local needs and conditions, but the task for any lower school remains constant: to serve students in their growth and development through childhood and beyond. This distinction is all-important for K–8 planners.

The learning theorists who define the instructional approach for elementary and middle grades schools are the same:

> *Learning is an active process in which learners construct new ideas or concepts based on their current/past knowledge. The curriculum should be organized in a spiral manner so that the student continually builds upon what they have already learned.*
>
> —Jerome Bruner, Toward a Theory of Instruction

> *Cognitive structures correspond to four stages of child development: sensorimotor (ages 0–2), preoperational–intuitive (ages 3–7), concrete operations–logical (ages 8–11), and formal operations–abstraction (ages 12–15). Any learning activities should involve the appropriate level of motor or mental operation for a child; avoid asking students to perform tasks that are beyond their current cognitive abilities.*
>
> —Jean Piaget, The Science of Education
> and the Psychology of the Child

> *Social interaction plays a fundamental role in the development of cognition. Full intellectual development requires social interaction.*
>
> —L. Vygotsky, Thought and Language

> *Significant learning takes place when the subject matter is relevant to the personal interests of the student; the student is the originator of learning.*
>
> —C. R. Rogers, Freedom to Learn

AN INITIAL LOOK AT THE NEW K–8 PROGRAM WE NEED

In districts that are restructuring education by creating K–8 schools, the question of what such a school might look like is an important one. Simply to combine grades or consolidate grades into a single school may invalidate nearly a century of knowledge about children and how they learn. Educators are aware, and accept the premise, that there are distinct growth periods within the 5–13-year-old age range. Even if all of these students are housed in only one facility, they cannot be offered a single unitary program. The curriculum of the K–8 school will necessarily be unique. Your author, who has worked with both elementary and intermediate schools for more than three decades, envisions some general organizers for any new K–8 program:

The school curriculum will

- be organized by distinct phases of development including, early childhood, late childhood, preadolescence, and adolescence,

- be concerned with general education and not simply academic specialization,
- be sequential in all subjects from orientation, to mastery, to expansion, and finally to application,
- define content in terms of required state learning standards, and
- use learning skills to create a seamless general education (K–8) experience for all students.

For more than one hundred years, American educators have studied the growth and development of young people. During the K–8 years in school, students will evolve from young children (ages 5–6) to older children (ages 7–10), to preadolescence (ages 11–12), and finally into adolescence (13+). The physical, social, intellectual, and emotional state of each student is different at each stage of development, and acknowledging these stages of growth will make any K–8 curriculum more relevant and effective.

By capping this new school at the eighth grade, designers will have the advantage of not being burdened by existing high school credit requirements (Carnegie units for graduation). In fact, in most states, there is little regulation of the curriculum prior to the ninth grade. As a result of this freedom, the K–8 school can develop a program that is organized in a logical way, one that benefits all students in attendance, and one that leads to a more functional level of citizenship regardless of the academic destination of the student. A "general education" for all students has always been one of the strengths of the public education system of the United States.

The curriculum of the K–8 school will be organized to meet the developmental needs of the student and will have four stages regardless of grade level or subject:

1. Orientation
2. Foundational learning
3. Expansion and exploration
4. Application

This simple progression follows all that is known about teaching and learning at this level of schooling.

Subject learning standards, developed by all states over the past decade, will help order this K–8 curriculum so that it will be a defined experience. All students should experience nine years of planned curriculum during Grades K–8, even if they do not completely master the entire curriculum. Any new K–8 school will have to accommodate the increasing range of student performance: As students progress through school, they spread out in level of attainment, achievement, and maturity, so that in any given class there will be a year of range in these levels for each year the students have

Figure 1.7   The learning progression in K–8 schools

Orientation → Foundational Learning → Exploration → Application

attended school (e.g., 1 year of range in reading in first grade, 4 years of range in reading in fourth grade). The K–8 school will need to plan for this range of learning in its performance standards, learning materials, classroom instruction, and student assessment.

Finally, what will make this new K–8 school seamless from kindergarten to eighth grade will be the way in which learning skills and thinking skills are used to treat subject content material. Each student, regardless of their achievement level in a given subject area, will learn to assess the knowledge and apply it in post-school life.

The curriculum models used by emerging K–8 schools are varied and represent the needs and priorities of the communities that support them.

- A Florida school in the Orlando area is using an integrated approach to make the curriculum meaningful to students. Citizenship skills and values are woven into all lessons.
- A K–8 on the Westside of Los Angeles promotes student security by emphasizing family groups and having all students participate in community service projects. First graders are paired with third graders for skill learning, and fifth graders and students from the kindergarten are paired for lessons in art, poetry, and celebrations.
- A school in suburban Maryland has adopted the K–8 model to halt a decline in academic performance. Special programs in language, the performing arts, Montessori, and academic magnets will be superimposed on regular school programs.
- A rural K–8 school in Oregon is beefing up its technology to help its students gain access to more advanced academic offerings.

SOME ISSUES ASSOCIATED WITH K–8 EDUCATION

The original K–8 program of the 19th and early 20th centuries was a terminal program of general education and citizenship. During the 20th century, the number of American students attending high school and beyond has grown dramatically. An initial issue for any K–8 school will be to deliver some sort of academic program that adequately prepares students for high school. For reasons listed throughout this chapter, many K–8 schools are not currently prepared to accomplish this task.

A second issue for the K–8 model will be to also deliver a curriculum that benefits older children and preadolescents. Creating K–8 schools by adding on grades means that the facility, faculty preparation, and instructional procedures will be primarily for an "elementary" program. Although much of the current literature on K–8 schools suggests that eleven-, twelve-, and thirteen-year-olds can be housed in an existing elementary school without much difficulty, the author finds the notion troubling. Preadolescent and adolescent students are full of energy, emotions, and social behaviors that will not easily be accommodated in the typical self-contained elementary classroom. The distinctive feature of this age group (11–13) is their puberty and all of its active manifestations. Somehow, a program for "growing up" will have to be developed and delivered within the K–8 structure.

Third, the role of subject content in the new K–8 school must be addressed and clarified. Some see this level as continued general education and other see this level as a preparation for secondary studies. Both the junior high school and the middle school attempted to ignore the strong philosophic differences about the purpose of education at this level and paid dearly for that omission. Clearly, this new K–8 school must stand on its own and do what is best for all of its students.

Finally, an issue for many new K–8 programs will be to keep focused on why this school is emerging, largely unplanned, in the United States at this time. Critics tell us that middle schools are doing a poor job with student achievement, discipline, and attitudes toward learning. Parents are pushing school boards to create a school where their child is safe and known by teachers, and where every student can experience success. Both the existing junior high school and the middle school have seemingly lost sight of these "forces for restructuring" and are disappearing rapidly. The new K–8 school must learn from the mistakes of these other programs and keep their decision-making criteria highly focused at all times.

The nuts and bolts of developing a K–8 program in the 21st century will take care of themselves. What is most important for the reader to gain from this chapter is that this is an opportunity for teachers, principals, superintendents, board members, and parents to get it right this time, once and for all.

QUESTIONS FOR STUDY GROUPS

1. What can the new K–8 school do for students that the other pattern (6–8) did not provide?

2. Why does the author think it is important that the K–8 school follow a progressive model?

3. What must the K–8 school do to meet academic expectations for older students?

4. How can student development be used to organize the curriculum?

5. What must be done to meet the needs and concerns of K–8 parents?

SUMMARY

The K–8 school, the new American K–8 school, has rushed upon the scene in schools and districts throughout America without policy or funding, and sometimes without even planning. This new model is testimony to the displeasure of parents and educators with the current pattern of elementary and middle schools.

The promise of the new school, based on experience in many large districts, suburban districts, and numerous smaller rural districts, is that this may be a superior organization for American education. Many measures of a successful school, from academic performance, to behavior, to the reception of parents, seem to be confirmed by early assessments.

Despite such affirmation, there are concerns and issues in developing the K–8 model regardless of whether this is a conversion or a brand new educational design. Those key issues include the academic program of the school, the need to service at least three developmental stages in one building, the accommodation of sometimes-difficult preadolescent learners, and staying focused on what parents and communities want from this new school.

The new K–8 school represents an opportunity to get it right this time. As such, the development of a curriculum program for this school may serve as a source of renewal for all involved in the process.

REFERENCES

Bruner, J. (1966). *Toward a theory of instruction*. Cambridge: Harvard University Press.

Elkind, D. (1981). *The hurried child: Growing up too fast too soon, reading*. Reading, MA: Addison-Wesley.

Elkind, D. (1994). *A sympathetic understanding of the child: Birth to sixteen* (3rd ed.). Boston: Allyn and Bacon.

Gardner, H. (2000). *Intelligence reframed: Multiple intelligences for the 21st century*. New York: Basic Books.

Gessell, F., & Gessell, A. (1946). *The child from five to ten*. New York: Harper.

Havighurst, R. (1962). *Society and education*. Boston: Allyn and Bacon.

Jones, H. E., & Bayley, N. (1962). The Berkeley growth study. *Child Development, 12*(2), 167–173.

Piaget, J., & Flavell, J. (1963). *Developmental psychology of Jean Piaget*. New York: Van Norstrand Reinhold.

Piaget, J. (1970). *The science of education and the psychology of the child*. New York: Grossman.

Rogers, C. (1969). *Freedom to learn*. Boston: Houghton-Mifflin.

Vygotsky, L. (1986). *Thought and language (revised edition)*. Cambridge: MIT Press.

Wiles, J. (1975, March). Middle school research 1968–1974: A review of substantial studies. *Educational Leadership*, pp. 421–423.

Using Standards to Define K–8 Programs

Curriculum standards are an essential planning element for a new K–8 program, regardless of whether the school is created from a conversion, a consolidation of schools, or a brand new design effort. By using learning standards as the parameters of the curriculum, what is to be taught can be clearly defined, and the traditional "gulf" between elementary and intermediate curricula can be effectively bridged. Traditionally weak academic performances in the middle grades can be overcome by clearly delineating the content and skills that belong in the elementary and intermediate levels. Students can experience relevant and continuous progress from kindergarten through eighth grade in the new K–8 school.

ORIGINS OF STANDARDS

For more than twenty-five years, American educators have been actively altering what is taught and tested in school. By 1998, forty-eight states and the District of Columbia had instituted some sort of standards-based curriculum. By 2000, twenty states had begun progression testing to assess mastery of learning standards; most assessing progress at Grades 4, 8, and 10. Obviously, a very major change has transpired in the school curriculum throughout our nation, and how such curriculum is developed.

What began as a simple demand for academic performance and cost accountability in education soon became an avalanche of curriculum reform in nearly every state. During the 1990s, the standards movement stimulated change in the very infrastructure of our schools (Eastin, 1998). Rigorous academic standards were developed, testing programs were instituted, and state legislatures demanded an extensive engineering of the curriculum. For the first time in the United States, the basic content that children must master in school at every grade level was explicitly spelled out by law.

Learning standards in schools have many valuable purposes that will be useful in designing the new K–8 school. These standards

- highlight the most important concepts and skills for each grade level,
- present a manageable number of concepts and skills for all students,
- help order the many concepts and skills over several grade levels,
- support assessment devices that determine that learning is occurring, and
- provide a means of integrating multiple subjects and skill areas.

For teachers, the standards can direct students to key concepts and skills, help communicate with parents and the community about educational priorities, and serve as decision-making criteria when planning lessons. Every teacher knows exactly what they are responsible for during classroom instruction. For administrators, learning standards provide a boundary for the curriculum itself, and an accountability measure in assessing teaching.

It is evident that all state learning standards are "minimum" standards that illuminate a general path to learning. These standards provide a detailed and coherent guide to content learning in all grades and should serve as a blueprint for steady academic progress for all students. Standards are especially helpful in Grades K–8 where, historically, there have been major gaps and redundancy in the curriculum. They should also assist in overcoming articulation (grade-to-grade) problems within and between the elementary and intermediate programs.

Educators interested in developing successful K–8 programs should invest the time and the effort to review and apply existing learning standards to any new K–8 program; much of what has been wrong with intermediate programs will soon disappear.

National Standards for K–8 Education

In 2002, the federal government enacted and signed into law the No Child Left Behind Act (NCLB), which required states to measure "adequate yearly progress." This adequate-yearly-progress provision (section 1111) called for states to set "challenging standards" in reading and mathematics by 2007–2008, and in science by 2014, and to align those standards with tests of progress for all students. According to NCLB, by the year 2014 all students must meet or exceed proficiency on state assessments in reading, mathematics, and science. Implied in this legislation was a loss of federal funding for any state not complying with this mandate.

As this book is written, the future of the NCLB legislation is in question. Because education is a state's right under our Constitution, it is unlikely that the courts would uphold a federal mandate for any change of this nature. Also, 47 states had lodged protests against the inadequate funding to mandate this law (about one-fourth of the funding needed to implement the bill was contributed by federal sources). Two states, Utah and Connecticut, filed lawsuits against the federal government in an effort to terminate the program. Finally, following the 2008 presidential election, it appears that the Obama administration may have other strategies for the improvement of public education in the land.

NCLB has been extremely effective in forcing states and school districts to develop basic learning standards. Once it became clear that individual states would pass laws to mandate learning standards for schools, national and international professional organizations jumped in to help conceptualize these content priorities.

One leading example of the contributions of these professional organizations is found in the work of the National Council of Teachers of Mathematics, an international organization that took the initiative to define math study for our schools. The first product of their work was *Curriculum and Evaluation Standards for School Mathematics* (1989), which clarified goals for math. This document was followed by *Professional Standards for Teaching Mathematics* (1991) and *Assessment Standards for School Mathematics* (1995). In 1997, NCTM initiated an effort to produce an electronic version of *Principles and Standards for School Mathematics* (1998), now available on its Web page at standards.nctm.org.

Following the lead of the NCTM, other subject groups also developed thoughtful learning standards for schools. These professionally developed standards have become the source of grade-level learning standards in most states.

Subject Matter Standards in K–8 Schools

As the reader reviews those learning standards developed by various professional organizations, it is obvious that most states have adopted these professional compilations without much editing. For this reason, competencies for mathematics will look similar in Washington, Florida, Massachusetts, and Arizona. The reader will also note that most of the associations that developed standards divided them up into grade levels or according to developmental stages (K–2, 3–5, 6–8). This is very useful for developing K–8 programs because these new schools will contain three or four distinct developmental stages.

For building-level leaders designing and implementing a K–8 curriculum, this ordering of state standards also means that teachers who are at the elementary level will probably be familiar with elementary standards, and those previously in middle schools will know intermediate standards. The teachers at either level may not, however, know the other level. The state and national learning standards can serve first as a communication device between these teachers from different levels in understanding the total K–8 mission.

A simple K–8 subject continuum from national and state standards for Grades K–8, in the basic subject areas, is presented in Figures 2.1 through 2.4. These simple standards continuums are sufficient to encourage early communication within a faculty about the basic content and the skills that must be taught in this new school. The standards included are for the subjects of mathematics, science, language arts, and social studies.

In viewing these compilations, the reader is encouraged to focus particular attention on Grades 5, 6, and 7. These are the critical grades that will web-together the previous elementary and intermediate curriculums to form the new K–8 curriculum. Remember, many schools at this level do not possess a clear content continuum in these grades. State standards will define the gaps in terms of tested skills and content.

In districts where there has previously been a K–5, 6–8 pattern, there may be a tendency to spend much of the fifth and sixth grade instructional time repeating the elementary skills and content that some students have not mastered. Leaders in such schools seemingly make a decision that they must help all students catch up before moving on to new and higher level material. Although it is true that in most American schools some students are below grade-level expectation by the end of elementary school, this condition should not be accepted as the rationale for the curriculum in the upper grades of the K–8 school.

When leaders of the new K–8 schools accept the reality that all students will *not* progress at the same rate (lock-step), grade-by-grade, they can free themselves to plan a different and more appropriate kind of curriculum for students. In particular, thinking skills can be used as an effective progress continuum for all students through Grades K–8. This concept is developed further in Chapter 3.

Figure 2.1 K–8 mathematics standards

K

1. Represent, compare, and order whole numbers.
2. Describe shapes and spaces.
3. Order objects by measurable attributes.

1

4. Develop an understanding of addition and subtraction facts and strategies.
5. Develop an understanding of whole number relationships including grouping.
6. Compose two-dimensional and three-dimensional geometric shapes.

2

7. Develop an understanding of base-ten numerations systems and place value.
8. Develop quick recall of multi-digit addition and subtraction facts.
9. Develop an understanding of linear measurement and skill in measuring.

3

10. Develop an understanding of multiplication and division strategies.
11. Develop an understanding of fractions and fraction equivalence.
12. Describe and analyze properties of two-dimensional shapes.

4

13. Develop quick recall of multiplication and related division facts.
14. Develop an understanding of decimals, including connections with fractions.
15. Develop an understanding of area and determine area in two-dimensional shapes.

5

16. Develop an understanding of fluency with division and whole numbers.
17. Develop fluency with addition and subtraction of fractions and decimals.
18. Describe three-dimensional shapes and analyze their properties.

6

19. Develop fluency in the multiplication and division of fractions and decimals.
20. Connect ratio and rates to multiplication and division.
21. Write and interpret mathematical expressions and equations.

(Continued)

(Continued)

7

22. Apply proportionality, including similarity.
23. Use formulas to determine areas and volumes of three-dimensional shapes.
24. Use rational numbers to solve linear equations.

8

25. Analyze and represent linear functions and solve linear equations.
26. Analyze two- and three-dimensional figures using distance and angle.
27. Analyze and summarize data sets.

Source: Adapted from Florida Department of Education Math Standards, (2004), Tallahassee.

Figure 2.2   K–8 science standards

K–2

1. Observe changes in the day and night sky.
2. Describe and measure weather changes.
3. Discover the differences between living and non-living things.
4. Explain how organisms interact with their physical environment.
5. Describe similarities and differences between plants and animals.
6. Recognize objects by their different characteristics.
7. Recognize sources of energy and their uses.

3–5

8. Explain cycles and patterns on Earth and in the solar system.
9. Describe the Earth's resources and how they can be preserved.
10. Analyze weather changes that occur over time.
11. Differentiate between the life cycles of various plants and animals.
12. Describe how change in the ecosystem affects the survival of animals.
13. Observe simple physical and chemical changes.
14. Describe the properties of light and sound energy.
15. Describe the forces that affect objects and their motion.
16. Describe how technology affects human life.

6–8

17. Describe how motion in the universe causes predictable cyclical events.
18. State the relationship of matter and gravitational force.
19. Describe how rocks and minerals are formed and classified.

20. Describe processes that contribute to the changing of the Earth's surface.
21. Explain cell functions in animals and plants.
22. Explain the reproduction processes of humans and other animals.
23. Describe how sunlight supports the life of organisms through photosynthesis.
24. Explain the extinction of species resulting from environmental changes.
25. Describe renewable and nonrenewable sources of energy and their management.
26. Describe conservation of resources and how it can be promoted by citizens.
27. Give examples of how technology developed by science affects quality of life.
28. Give examples of inventions that have resulted from scientific inquiry.
29. Provide a list of factors that contribute to better health.
30. Describe the relationship of the U.S. Space program to societal improvement.

Source: Adapted from standards from Ohio, California, Arizona, and Michigan.

Figure 2.3   K–8 language arts standards

K

1. Discuss ideas and dictate a story.
2. Write capital and lowercase letters of the alphabet.
3. Follow simple oral directions, and share ideas in complete sentences.

1

4. Find title, author, and table of contents in a text.
5. Identify and describe a plot, setting, and characters of a story.
6. Write a complete sentence using spacing, plurals, and punctuation.

2

7. Identify common synonyms, antonyms, and compound words.
8. Make cause–effect connections from words such as first, next, and last.
9. Write and identify nouns and verbs in complete sentences.

3

10. Read aloud with appropriate timing and change in voice.
11. In a passage summarize the main idea and supporting details.
12. Write sentences of a variety of types (i.e., statements, commands, questions).

(Continued)

(Continued)

4

13. Use knowledge of root words and context clues to determine the meaning of words.
14. Describe cause and effect of character actions in stories.
15. Write simple and compound sentences using descriptive words and phrases.

5

16. Use features and organization (graphs) to aid in understanding text.
17. Use words that connect ideas within sentences (e.g., however, therefore).
18. Use gestures and phrasing to emphasize main points and enhance meaning.

6

19. Compare and contrast structural features of informational texts.
20. Analyze how figurative language creates tone and meaning in literary texts.
21. Identify persuasive techniques in speeches and presentations.

7

22. Use Greek, Latin, and Anglo-Saxon roots to understand vocabulary.
23. Describe relationship of setting, mood, tone, and plot in literary works.
24. Develop persuasive speeches, summaries, and research for particular purposes.

8

25. Identify the difference between the literal and figurative meaning of words.
26. Use graphic organizers and strategies to plan writing.
27. Write paragraphs that display varied sentence construction.

Source: Adapted from Indiana Department of Education, Language Arts Standards (2008). Retrieved February 20, 2008, from http://dc.doe.in.gov/Standards/Academic Standards/index.shtml

Figure 2.4   K–8 social studies standards

K–2

1. Place events in correct order on a time line.
2. Compare daily life in the past and in the present.
3. Read stories about how diverse backgrounds have influenced America.
4. Identify practices and products of diverse cultures.

---

5. Identify the location of our state, the USA, and other continents.
6. Identify physical and human features of places.
7. Explain how environment influences human activity.
8. Explain how resource scarcity requires choices to satisfy wants.
9. Distinguish between goods and services.
10. Identify elected leaders and authority figures in the community.
11. Recognize and explain symbols of the United States.
12. Explain the purpose of rules in different settings.
13. Construct time lines to demonstrate chronological order.

3–5

14. Describe cultural patterns evident in North America.
15. Explain the consequences of interaction between cultural groups.
16. Use map elements to identify places and regions in North America.
17. Explain how transportation and communication relate to economic activity.
18. Explain how competition affects producers and consumers in a market.
19. Identify the responsibilities of branches of the U.S. government.
20. Give examples of documents that structure government in a democracy.
21. Explain how citizens participate in civic life to promote the common good.
22. Identify important rights and responsibilities of citizenship in the U.S.

6–8

23. Explain causes and consequences of the American Revolution.
24. Analyze the causes and consequences of the American Civil War.
25. Compare and contrast cultural practices of past civilizations.
26. Explain how contact between cultures impacts belief systems.
27. Identify on a map the location of human features on each continent.
28. Explain how trade occurs and how trade contributes to global interdependence.
29. Identify connections between government policies and the economy.
30. Compare the characteristics of democracies, monarchies, and dictatorships.

Source: Adapted from Ohio Department of Education Standards.

Also of importance in today's new K–8 school is the way in which technology is embedded in the curriculum. Figure 2.5 presents the suggested standards to be mastered by students in Grades K–8.

Technology should play a very major role in any new K–8 school, particularly in the upper grades, by helping teachers to tailor or individualize instruction for all students. The availability of software today ranges from remedial to extended study, and much of it is free to schools, students,

Figure 2.5   K–8 technology standards

K–2

1. Use input devices (mouse, keyboard) and output devices (monitor, printer).
2. Use media resources for directed and independent learning.
3. Communicate about technology using accurate terminology.
4. Use multimedia resources, such as online encyclopedias, to support learning.
5. Work collaboratively with peers through technology.
6. Demonstrate ethical behaviors when using technology.
7. Create multimedia products.
8. Use multimedia tools and software for problem solving.

3–5

9. Gather information and communicate with others.
10. Discuss uses of technology in everyday life, citing advantages and disadvantages.
11. Describe personal consequences for the inappropriate use of technology.
12. Use tools and peripherals to remediate skill deficits and support productivity.
13. Use technological tools for individual communication and publishing products.
14. Use e-mail, chats, and blogs to participate in collaborative problem solving.
15. Use technology (digital cameras and scanners) for extended learning activities.
16. Be able to select the appropriate technology to address tasks and solve problems.
17. Evaluate the appropriateness and biases of electronic information sources.

6–8

18. Apply strategies for solving routine hardware and software problems.
19. Demonstrate knowledge of current changes in information technology.
20. Discuss the application of new technologies to the everyday workplace.
21. Use content specific tools (Web tools, graphing calculators) to support learning.
22. Design, develop, and publish resources using technology for export.
23. Collaborate with peers and experts using telecommunication.
24. Demonstrate an understanding of connectivity and provide practical applications.
25. Research the accuracy of electronic information sources in real world usage.

Source: These standards adapted from those produced by Bellingham, Washington, Sioux City, South Dakota, Los Gatos USD, and the Michigan Educational Tech Standards. Adapted from National Educational Technology Standards (2008), *Los Gatos Union District technology integration vision.* Retrieved February 20, 2009, from www.lgusd.k12.ca.us/curriculum/technology/documents/DigLitGoals2007-2012.pdf

and their parents. For example, girls seem to have difficulty scoring on mathematics achievement tests during the intermediate grades for many reasons. Figure 2.6 provides a sampling of free Web sites that might be used to solve this instructional problem.

Figure 2.6   Helpful Web sites for teaching mathematics to girls

A complete content curriculum for mathematics K–12	http://mathforum.org/mathtools
Math lessons and plans for all levels	www.mathsearch.com/arithmetic
North Carolina public schools curriculum for math	http://www.ncpublicschools.org/curriculum/
Worksheets, puzzles, test prep for math, all levels	http://www.edhelper.com/math.htm
Math questions? Ask the experts. E-mail contact with professors	http://www.mathforum.org/dr.math
Helping girls in math, assessment and tutoring Grades 3–12	http://www.maa.org

Comparable sites are available for language arts, science, social studies, and even foreign languages. The reader will note that, unlike a classroom teacher, the computer holds the promise of developing a personalized curriculum simultaneously for an infinite number of students. Just like a personal telephone number, students can receive a personal learning program in school. What must be considered by planners in developing the K–8 school is how much common instructional delivery will be provided by classroom teachers and how much technological delivery of a personalized curriculum can be provided via the Internet.

EXTENDING STANDARDS IN K–8 SCHOOLS

Whereas academic standards and achievement testing will be a large part of defining any K–8 school curriculum, educators and parents must remember that traditional elementary and intermediate curricula are far more than minimal achievement standards. Both elementary and intermediate educators have historically believed in a broad and general education program. Educators at the elementary and intermediate level also perceive children as active learners accommodating new knowledge through restructuring information and constructing knowledge in new ways. The connectionism of John Dewey's time and the constructivist theory of today hold that the student (not the teacher) is the center of the learning process because it is the student who applies meaning to information. Beyond just knowing things, and scoring well on tests, students in K–8 schools must be able to use knowledge and learning skills in their daily lives.

K–8 schools use learning standards in a number of creative ways to improve the learning program, as shown by the examples below.

- The Boston Public Schools use learning standards to insure that each school follows the prescribed curriculum. This practice eases the student transfers between K–8 schools.
- In Whitesboro, New York, the curriculum taught is placed on the district Web page so that parents can monitor student studies.
- In Illinois, K–8 schools follow new emotional development standards to enhance students' school readiness and ability to achieve academic success.
- Anchorage, Alaska K–8 schools use social and emotional learning standards to teach students self-management, social awareness, and sensitivity to inclusion programs.

LEARNING TARGETS FOR STANDARDS-BASED SCHOOLS

Standards can help define the basic program of the new K–8 school, but there is much more to the curriculum of the K–8 school than learning standards. As previously mentioned, this new school will contain three or four distinct periods of human development, and during these periods of growth, students will be preoccupied with what sociologist Robert Havighurst has called "developmental tasks" (Havighurst, 1962). Students in K–8 schools will attend to these personal tasks in the act of growing up, and the K–8 school program can hinder or facilitate these actions. When students can serve their own needs through planned school tasks, they will always be involved and motivated. Conversely, if the school does not allow the students to attend to these tasks of development, discipline problems may ensue. Examples of these developmental tasks are found in Figure 2.7.

An understanding of what is really "basic" in the K–8 school might come from the work of the Swiss educator Jean Piaget, who describes cognitive development (thinking) in young people during similar developmental stages.

Figure 2.7 Developmental tasks of the three periods

Early Childhood

Developing motor control

Emerging self-awareness

Mapping our surroundings

Assigning meaning to events

Developing relationships with others

Developing language and thought patterns

Middle Childhood

Structuring the physical world

Refining language and thought patterns

Establishing relationships with others

Understanding sex roles

Later Childhood

Mastering communication skills

Building meaningful peer relationships

Thinking independently

Acceptance of self

Finding constructive outlets for self-expression

Role projection

Preadolescence

Handling major body changes

Asserting independence from the family

Establishing sex role identity

Dealing with peer relations

Controlling emotions

Constructing a values foundation

Expanding personal interests

Using new reasoning capacities

Developing an acceptable self-concept

Source: Jon Wiles (2005), *Curriculum Essentials, 2nd edition,* Boston: Allyn & Bacon. Used by permission.

1. In the first stage (*Sensorimotor* period, 0–2 years) very young children react to their environment through reflex, habit formation, object identification, active experimentation, and the beginnings of symbolic representation.

2. In a second stage of cognitive development (*Preoperational* period, 2–7 years), which includes the first 2 years of schooling, children learn to represent objects with images and words and to develop language skills. They are highly imaginative, engage in preliminary problem solving, and use imitative learning.

3. In the third period (*Concrete operational* period, 7–11), or Grades 2–5, children become skillful at classifying and using logic. What distinguishes this period is the absence of abstract reasoning; children can problem-solve using concrete objects, but have difficulty with hypothetical or conceptual problems.

4. In the fourth period (*Formal operations*, 11+), beginning around the sixth grade, a time that is tied to puberty, the student gains the capacity to think in abstraction, develop conceptual values, and can make adult-like connections from highly disparate information; they can think! These new developmental capacities are physiological, psychosexual, and psychosocial in nature.

The important contribution of Jean Piaget is the idea that the student who is entering the upper grades of a K–8 school will, through simple natural development, become capable of higher-order thinking and the application of content to real world problems and issues. Because puberty occurs between ages 10 and 14 for 95% of American children, this "new capacity" will happen while students are in the K–8 school. And, this change will occur because of nature—simple developmental maturation—not because of teaching or previous school learning.

Another view of what might be considered basic, and of how standards for learning might be adapted in a K–8 school, comes from the National Task Force on Minority Achievement, who issued their report, *Reaching the Top* (1999) in response to low test performances by minority children. The report defined *academic ability* by capabilities such as

- literacy and numeracy,
- mathematical and verbal reasoning,
- skill in creating, recognizing, and resolving relationships,
- problem solving, abstract and concrete, using deductive and inductive reasoning,
- sensitivity to multiple contexts and perspectives,

- skill in accessing and assessing disparate bodies of information,
- seeking help through resource recognition and utilization, and
- self-regulation.

These academic skills are rarely taught in isolation, but rather result from the student being able to "take control" of learning and become academically empowered. Because all twenty-one of the large school districts moving to K–8 schools have extensive minority populations, this prescription seems particularly relevant for curriculum planners.

Another target for the possible application of standards in a K–8 school is the world of work, a near destination for the nearly one-third of K–8 students who will not complete high school.

The authoritative guide in this topic area is the SCANS report (U.S. Department of Labor, 1991) titled *What Work Requires of Schools.* This report notes that all American students must develop a new set of competencies and foundational skills if they are to enjoy a productive, full, and satisfying life. Regardless of whether a student leaves school to start work, be an apprentice, go into the armed services, go to college, or become married, they need to possess foundational work skills. These would include

- basic skills such as reading, writing, computation, mathematics, and speaking,
- thinking skills such as making decisions, solving problems, knowing how to learn, and reasoning, and
- personal qualities such as individual responsibility, self-esteem, sociability, integrity, and self-management.

In addition, this report calls for learning to work on teams, serving customers, leading, working with people from culturally diverse backgrounds, using computers to process data, understanding organizations, evaluating data, allocating time, monitoring and correcting performance, and a host of other small skills useful in any workplace:

American students will leave grades four, eight, and twelve having demonstrated competency in challenging subject matter, including English, mathematics, and science—and every school in America will ensure that all students use their minds so they will be prepared for responsible citizenship—and employment in our modern society. Every adult will be competent and will possess the knowledge and skills necessary to compete in the global economy. (U.S. Department of Labor, 1991)

Finally, another possible prescription for applying standards in K–8 schools is a list of what successful students do to succeed in the secondary school. This list was developed by a group of Michigan teachers for a Kellogg Foundation program by working backwards from high school. In the eyes of these teachers, successful students monitored academic goals, accepted responsibility, possessed solid self-esteem, were organized, and exhibited positive attitudes and enthusiasm for learning. These "outcomes" are delineated in Figure 2.8.

As we look at these five examples of "goals" for applied learning standards, we can see that in any K–8 school, the minimal learning standards

Figure 2.8   Behavioral goals for students completing eighth grade

Responsibility

Arrive on time
Increased sensitivity to needs of others
Voluntary assistance to others in need
Exhibit awareness of health

Self-esteem

Increased openness to new experiences
Elimination of self-abusive behaviors
Exhibit pride in self and school

Organization

Bring materials to class
Complete work
Maintain personal calendar
Manage time wisely
Ask questions to clarify responsibility

Attitudes

Ability to introduce self to others
Know etiquette
Dress neatly and appear well-groomed
Participate in school activities
Exhibit enthusiasm for learning

Source: "Goals for Student Behavior," in Jon Wiles (2005), *Curriculum Essentials, 2nd Edition.* Boston: Allyn & Bacon. Used by permission.

are not ends, but are actually means to larger and more lasting goals. Whether we are helping students master developmental growth tasks, develop higher thinking skills, prepare for success in later learning, get ready for the world of work, or just be a better and more highly organized individuals, these should be the real and measurable outcomes of K–8 education. Learning standards may make the K–8 curriculum smoother, more defined, and more logical, but they are inadequate to serve as the *curriculum*.

MANAGING STANDARDS-BASED PROGRAMS

There is no question that as long as the standards-based movement in the United States is viable and supported by state laws, educators have little choice but to manage them as they are mandated. In Florida, for instance, Florida Statute 1006.34(2)(b) states "Content must align with the state's standards for the subject, grade level, and learning outcomes." Clearly the *what* part of the curriculum has been determined in many states of our nation. However, it is *how* the curriculum is treated and delivered that determines the meaning of that curriculum. Therefore, designing instruction at the classroom level in K–8 schools, around mandated standards, becomes of highest importance to school leaders. To allow the K–8 school to be simply routinized, like some 19th century factory, is to abandon more than a century of professional knowledge and consensus about teaching and learning in our lower grades. Leaders must follow the standards-based curriculum into the classroom to insure its validity and relevance for students.

Managing the curriculum at the classroom level would involve the following concerns.

1. Insuring proper resources

2. Aligning the various instructional components

3. Organizing instruction materials

4. Checking for developmental appropriateness

5. Helping teachers pace content

6. Addressing student motivation

Being sure that teachers have adequate resources has become a huge problem in the era of standards-based education. In some commercial programs, such as *America's Choice*, project leaders sought to replace textbooks with special paper learning packets keyed to the mastery of content and skills. When such programs terminate or fail, districts can be left with no libraries and no texts for learning.

A more common problem is that the materials in a standards-based curriculum are not comprehensive enough to accommodate all of the learners in attendance. A rule-of-thumb in education planning is that for each year in school, there is one year of *range*. In fourth grade, for example, there would be a four-year reading range. Materials should be available to engage students where they are, but it is common in the standards-based programs to have only uniform learning materials at the level of the objective.

Materials used in the classroom should integrate reference aids such as maps, pictures, glossaries, and bibliographies, but often these are absent. The classroom curriculum, in some standards-based programs, is presented without context or references. Enrichment or remediation materials are rarely present in state-mandated curriculum materials, since all children are expected to perform at a predetermined grade level. Readability of the materials often goes well beyond the level of student comprehension.

The degree to which the materials are colorful, relevant, and interesting to the age group has a lot to do with student performance on a state test. In many states, resources must reflect an identifiable skill emphasis like "problem solving" to be adopted as a resource.

The scope of study, and the sequencing of materials, is a valuable contribution of any standards-based curriculum. Tying those organized outcomes to classroom materials, however, requires considerable thought. The "integrity of a curriculum," its structure and logical organization, is often torn apart by the testing expectations of standards-based systems. For teachers to skip over parts of the curriculum known to not be tested is to present the student with a fragmented course of study and a game show mentality toward scholarship. Narratives and visuals are often left out of highly focused state curricula.

Working to keep the concept of "developmental appropriateness" in front of teachers constitutes a difficult task for curriculum leaders because such an idea is nonexistent in the standards-based curriculum. State legislation rarely addresses the capacity of children at developmental levels. Clearly, eight-year-olds do not have the knowledge or the cognitive ability to compare and contrast Eastern and Western cultures in the Renaissance period (Florida standards for third graders). Children of any age can learn almost any concept if it is taught in some legitimate form, but the school leader must be prepared to help teachers translate state standards using educational logic.

Helping teachers pace the delivery of the curriculum is an important role for leaders in the new K–8 school. Many states have moved forward their date for starting school in order to get more study time in before spring testing. Helping teachers articulate the curriculum from year to year, and minimize summer losses by students, is an important task of leadership. Also, insuring that subject matter and skills are organized around concepts or even "chunks" of knowledge is important for long-term learning.

Finally, and a massive task for K–8 leaders, is to help teachers address learning theory and student motivation. On testing day in many states, school children experience a wide variety of sickness and test anxiety based on unrealistic test expectations by parents, teachers, and administrators. Such fear and anxiety suppresses test performance and begins a cycle of failure and despair for the student, his teacher, the school, and the district. The best preparation for any standardized test is confidence, understanding, and test motivation. Obviously, in many of the high-stakes testing states, a dropout rate of more than 35% does not speak well for the current procedures.

The North Central Regional Educational Laboratory (NCREL, 2004) identified conditions which must be promoted in order to serve all children in K–8 public schools. The two sets of skills, nurturing intellectual competence and promoting the transfer of knowledge, help translate learning to the real world.

NURTURING INTELLECTUAL COMPETENCE

The modern constructivist view of the teaching–learning act holds that the child is an active participant in making sense of the world. From this vantage point, the world is a laboratory for all of us, and we bring to learning what we already know about life. Students are not empty minds to be filled, but rather participants with background and prior knowledge. Possessing intellectual competence, from this perspective, is far more than "knowing." Competence is defined by the use of what is known. Certain teaching strategies help to activate knowledge that the learner already possesses or is presently acquiring.

Among the generic skills of teaching that would assist a learner in becoming more intellectually competent would be learning how to acquire new knowledge, consolidating and conceptualizing what is already known, gaining deep structural understandings, and seeing connectivity in information.

Learning to acquire new information is generally a process of taking what is known or is being learned and placing it in a context or construct that orders it. Inquiry-based and problem-solving approaches using questions or proofs generally force the student to fit information into preconceived theories or preconceptions. While these "fits" may not be precise, they promote connecting knowledge. Consolidating or "placing knowledge" is important to overcome randomness in learning.

Learning skills (such a diagramming or math problems) and practice can routinize the act of learning. Just as a frequent reader becomes more proficient with practice, learning to summarize or to understand knowledge is a sort of shorthand for learning.

Deep understanding is a conceptual level at which much information can be summarized by a thought or symbol that shapes the learning episode. Active (or authentic) learning and problem-based learning both contribute to this deeper understanding. Such learning can especially help children whose view of life may already be heavily influenced by their parents' nonconventional perceptions or previous experience.

Transfer or connectivity of information is the final subskill contributing to intellectual competence. This skill involves taking learning in one context and moving it to another context. Teacher modeling and suggestion play a big role in this kind of learning. Teacher questions and activity can structure such transfer for the student.

TRANSFER OF KNOWLEDGE

Students are sent to school to learn things, acquire skills, and develop abilities that will serve them in later life—not to simply pass a standardized test! During the past one hundred years, there have been numerous pedagogic approaches that have reflected our best understanding about how to use knowledge. These practices must be applied in today's classroom in order to make the standardized curriculum valuable.

Among the best known ideas in this regard are that (a) specific knowledge cannot be too contextualized if transfer is to occur, (b) knowledge transfer is an active not a passive process, and (c) the design of instruction must reflect the notion that the child possesses previous knowing. These three ideas can be illustrated in basic learning approaches that would promote transfer of learning.

To help the student overcome what is too often a totally contextualized environment in standards-based learning, teachers should allow students to practice retrieval of information and formation of that knowledge in their own words. Teachers should also encourage the representation of knowledge in alternative forms. To encourage student behavior as an active participant, teachers should build on student's prior knowledge and background, infuse lessons with strategies for learning, and vary the conditions of learning. Finally, to reflect that the student is an associative learner, teachers should use alternative assessment and emphasize skill development as well as knowledge acquisition.

QUESTIONS FOR STUDY GROUPS

1. What is to be taught in Grades 5–7 using your state's standards?

2. Should all students progress together grade-by-grade or should they progress at their own rate following a common continuum of learning?

3. How much of the curriculum should be delivered in standardized form in the classroom, and how much should be delivered personalized to each individual via the Internet?

4. What is the role of the student in learning?

5. What are the capabilities of students at various developmental stages?

6. Can all students be expected to perform at a predetermined grade level?

SUMMARY

Curriculum standards are an essential element in planning a K–8 school. The standards will help bridge the now existing gulf between elementary and intermediate programs in most districts. The use of learning standards in Grades 5–8 should increase the academic performance of any K–8 school.

Learning standards should be viewed by those planning K–8 schools as minimal requirements for all students, not as "the curriculum." In particular, those standards that address only subject-matter competence are incomplete and do not mandate a delivery method. The author believes that how the curriculum is delivered to students will determine its meaning to the student. Technology, for example, holds tremendous promise in K–8 schools for meeting individual student learning needs.

Leaders of K–8 schools looking for the bigger picture will find goals in student developmental patterns, prescriptions for success after school, learning needed for the world of work, and behaviors thought critical in success after formal school.

Leaders can bring the many learning standards to life by working with teachers in the classroom in implementing standards. In particular, teachers need to help students develop intellectual competence and to transfer knowledge to real world settings.

REFERENCES

Bellingham Public Schools. (2009). *Bellingham Washington standards.* Retrieved February 20, 2009, from http://www.bham.wednet.edu/technology/technology .htm

Eastin, D. (1998). *A message from the State Board of Education and the State Superintendent of Public Instruction.* Sacramento, CA: California Department of Education.

Havighurst, R. (1962). *Growing up in River City.* New York: Wiley & Sons.

North Central Regional Educational Laboratory. (2004). *Understanding the No Child Left Behind Act of 2001: Scientifically based research.* Retrieved February 20, 2009, from http://www.centerforcsri.org/

National Council of Teachers of Mathematics. (1989). *Curriculum and evaluation standards for school mathematics.* Reston, VA: Author.

National Council of Teachers of Mathematics. (1991). *Professional standards for teaching mathematics.* Reston, VA: Author.

National Council of Teachers of Mathematics. (1995). *Assessment Standards for School Mathematics.* Accessed May 13, 2009, at http://www.nctm.org/ standards/default.aspx?id=58

National Council of Teachers of Mathematics. (1998). *Principles and standards for school mathematics.* Reston, VA: Author.

National Task Force on Minority High Achievement. (1999). *Reaching the top.* New York: The College Board. (ERIC Document Reproduction Service No. ED438380)

U.S. Department of Labor. (1991, June). *What work requires of schools (SCANS Report for America 2000).* Washington, DC: National Technical Information Services, Department of Commerce.

Using Skills to Create the Seamless Curriculum

For nearly a century, educators in the upper elementary and middle school grades (5–7) have grappled with how to deal with the range of achievement and ability in students as they progress through schools. There is approximately a year of range in achievement, maturity, knowledge, and experience for each year in school up and through the eighth grade; after the eighth grade, the dropout rate narrows the range. In the past, educators have addressed this widening range of ability by repeating the curriculum, waiting for laggards, or by using ability grouping to create, in effect, two different classrooms within these grades. The author believes that none of these historic responses is acceptable in developing the new K–8 school curriculum.

Planners of the new K–8 curriculum will need to acknowledge that a content-driven curriculum, using the subject standards and testing as the measures of achievement, will produce the same results: that is, too many intermediate students not succeeding. This issue has plagued intermediate education for a century. A new and different approach is needed if the K–8 school is to succeed and flourish, and the beginning point for breaking this dilemma is to focus on the ends of education rather than the means. Subject matter content and learning skills are the means by which we achieve the ends of education. The end of education, the true purpose, is much larger than the simple mastery of core knowledge.

TWO CONCEPTIONS OF ENDS

There are many statements of goals for education in the elementary and middle schools. One such list, by Melvin Freestone (Freestone, 2006), sees the goals as five outcomes.

1. Being democratic

2. Being ethical

3. Being knowledgeable

4. Being imaginative

5. Being empowered

A successful student of any K–8 school would emerge from the program with democratic behaviors such as being able to work constructively with others, contributing to the community in which they live, making informed economic decisions, and being socially responsible. Each of these behaviors requires intelligent thought and a substantial understanding of the concepts found in school subjects.

An ethical student completing the K–8 school would have developed a degree of moral autonomy and would understand that values are implicit in most social decisions. Such a person would be able to explore and evaluate ideas and transcend cultural, religious, and socioeconomic differences in making personal decisions. Again, intelligent thought and a deep understanding of social information and ethical concepts would distinguish this K–8 graduate.

In today's digital world general information and ordered knowledge are overly plentiful. Students are awash in information from television, computers, texting, cell phones, the radio, and other electronics. The traditional role of knowledge has been reconfigured by the sheer volume of knowledge available to all people each day.

Traditionally, knowledge has provided a kind of perspective needed to make sense of our everyday experiences and at some level it still does. But the true value of knowledge today is found in its utility, and simply knowing things is no longer distinctive or adequate preparation for life after the school years. We must learn to see patterns in the volume of information, patterns that can guide everyday living. Informed actions result from the exercise of knowledge and understanding its relevant application.

Being imaginative goes hand-in-hand with living in a modern world. Massive changes in science and technology, and complex issues such as global warming and energy management, require each citizen to be flexible and imaginative in dealing with problems for living. Being imaginative requires both creativity and analytical critical-thinking skills, particularly in a futuristic nation like the United States.

Finally, a successful graduate of any K–8 school should exit the program empowered to act resourcefully in response to unforeseen or predictable changes. Empowerment can be defined as being able to direct one's own life and respond positively to problems and opportunities. Empowerment means a life that is satisfying and contains a sense of achievement. Intelligent thinking and insightful understanding are required.

Citizens that act democratically, are ethical in their behavior, are knowledgeable about life, evidence creativity and flexibility, and are empowered to act responsibly are the desired outcome of schooling as "general education." These traits transcend various circumstances, needs, and change and are foundational to our society now and in the future. Subject matter, learning skills, and related school experiences contribute to these ends.

A second new and relevant list of worthy goals for curriculum in K–8 schools has been provided by the Partnership for 21st Century Skills (2008), who offer a comprehensive outline of what might be needed. This statement addresses life and career skills, core content, and learning skills for the 21st century. This curricular prescription is being field-tested in the public schools of Iowa, Kansas, Maine, Massachusetts, New Jersey, North Carolina, South Dakota, West Virginia, and Wisconsin as this book is written.

Key life skills advocated by the Partnership include the following:

1. Flexibility and adaptability

2. Initiative and self-direction

3. Social and cross-cultural skills

4. Productivity and accountability

5. Leadership and responsibility

These skills would be taught within the standard K–8 content curriculum of English, foreign languages, arts, mathematics, economics, science, geography, history, and government or civics. In addition to the standard curriculum, the Partnership recommends global awareness, financial literacy, civic literacy, and health literacy. The curriculum advocated by the Partnership would teach these thinking, problem-solving, and communication skills "within the context of core subjects and 21st century interdisciplinary themes." This business and education leadership group also advocates a competency-based approach to learning, integration of new technologies into instruction, and using community resources beyond the school walls (Partnership, 2008).

One of the most important contributions of both of these conceptions of a new school curriculum is the role of subject matter or content in any new curriculum. Subjects are seen as interconnected, not as isolated disciplines of study as in the high school, and both prescriptions encourage deep understanding rather than the accumulation of shallow knowledge bases. Finally, both prescriptions allow for multiple measures of assessment as students learn to "use" knowledge regardless of their level of achievement or maturation. These conceptions place skills of learning at the center of the curriculum.

THE CURRICULUM DESIGN TASKS

The primary planning task for leaders of new K–8 programs is to conceptualize the desired outcomes for the first 9 years of schooling, and during this process, applied life skills, not content, should be seen as the common denominator for all students. In doing so, the K–8 program escapes the century-old tug-of-war between progressives and traditionalists and instantly becomes the new and appropriate curriculum for the 21st century in America.

The intersection of these 21st century skills with the traditional curriculum can take many different forms. It is probable that the most effective format for infusing these skills into classroom practices at various grade levels will be defined by the developmental stage of the learners. This means that the curriculum organization in the K–8 school may have multiple formats depending on the grade levels to which this strategy is applied. A model of how these applications might differ by developmental stage is offered by the author in Table 3.1.

The reader may wish to think for a moment about how a core skill such as problem solving might be taught at the first, fifth, and eighth grades. From our previous generic model for the curriculum, the first graders would be at an orientation level, the fifth graders at a foundational or mastery level, and the eighth graders at an application level.

First graders might explore electricity in their classroom by simple trial and error techniques. Fifth graders might be using the scientific method to explore the presence of electrons in the classroom. Eighth graders may be constructing a yet-to-be-invented machine for extracting methane hydrates from below the earth's surface. All are learning the skills of problem solving, but at different levels of sophistication and using different knowledge bases.

The seamless nature of the K–8 curriculum results from each student interacting with the content curriculum using a continuum of thinking skills appropriate to 21st century living. This is a major change from

Table 3.1 Curriculum organization model

Grades	Approach	Strategy	Assessment	Goal
Grades K–1 (Ages 5–6)	Orientation	Activities and conceptual learning	Participation and demonstration	Readiness
Grades 2–5 (Ages 7–10)	Direct instruction and skills mastery	Foundational core mastery content/skills	Standards mastery	Basic literacy
Grades 6–7 (Ages 11–12)	Exploration and expansion	Minimum-maximum curriculum	Portfolio	Growth and personal development
Grade 8 (13+)	Applications to adult living	Service learning and career settings	Portfolio and state standards	Preparation for adult living

curriculum designs of the past. Student learning will always occur in a context, and students in the K–8 school will engage subject matter with different backgrounds, motivations, and levels of readiness. By using learning skills to interact with that content, each student will naturally develop strategies and processes for later life that work for them.

For example, students learning about interest rates in mathematics can use skills of calculation at many levels of sophistication. One student might be calculating the interest on his or her passbook saving account at the bank, whereas another student in the same class might be working with bonds issued by Fannie Mae or Freddie Mac agencies. Both students are learning to calculate, but using different information for their practice.

In planning classroom learning experiences, various life themes, core subject content, and learning skills will be mixed into the lessons. Learning experiences in the K–8 school will be most meaningful to individual students when they do the following:

1. Link to their prior experiences or interests

2. Build on their existing understandings

3. Appear relevant to the lives they are currently living

4. Are shared with others in collaborative settings

5. Require application to real issues and challenges

If, for instance, an eighth grade student is studying American literature and reads Stephan Crane's *The Red Badge of Courage*, the teacher can help the student understand the lesson better by linking the story to the life of students today. Groups of students discussing the horror of a young man caught in a brutal war might easily liken the condition to teenagers and gang battles. Helping each student to define courage through this kind of medium would simultaneously help each student in his or her developmental task of self-definition.

Teachers who guide K–8 students along a path of orientation, mastery, expansion, and application will be answering basic "what," "how," and "why" questions for the learners. Under the teacher's guidance, the students will discover the presence of knowledge, examine it for purpose, learn its structure, determine how it is connected to other things, and find its utility in the real world beyond school. From such study will come a larger understanding of "big ideas" that will carry the learner into the future as a truly educated individual.

Some of the "big ideas" that organize the subject content in a K–8 school are found in Figure 3.1.

Figure 3.1 Big ideas found in content areas

Science	energy, matter, living things, earth and space, scientific inquiry
Social studies	government, law, citizenship, historical perspective, economic systems
Language arts	reading, writing, speaking, listening, understanding
Mathematics	size and shapes, numeracy, simple and complex operations, mental computations, relationships, ratios
Arts	music, visual art, dance, drama, perspective
Personal growth	physical wellness, emotional wellness, mental wellness

Such big ideas are contained in all subject matter and are activated by the individual student giving personal meaning to these academic perspectives by treating them through study. The student may ask, for example, what is math, how does math work, and what is math for? To answer these questions is to gain an understanding, at some level of sophistication, about the discipline of mathematics (Bruner, 1962). The use, or relevance, of math in the life of the student will depend on how the student thinks about this subject. As the school arms the student with thinking skills, knowledge becomes more valuable.

The seamless curriculum in the K–8 school will help each student to gain increasing amounts of understanding by using thinking skills to examine or treat the subject matter. This ability to assess subject content, and use it in a variety of personal ways, is the true essence of the seamless K–8 curriculum. School subjects can serve as the medium for study and learning, but not as the desired end of education.

In the K–8 school, because of the range of developmental stages and the diversity of the students, it can be expected that no two students will ever gain exactly the same understanding from the curriculum. They never have!

Students will master the state-tested content standards and will experience the seamless skill-treatments of the K–8 curriculum, but they will never draw a completely standardized conclusion from the lessons taught. Nor will they use the knowledge they have gained in school in exactly the same manner as adults. The task for planners of the K–8 school is to help all students learn and experience the most important applications of subjects and skills. Each student, regardless of his or her achievement level, will benefit from this kind of general education and emerge as a more functional citizen.

Students who complete the K–8 curriculum should emerge as self-directed learners who can gather information, define issues, make judgments, devise alternatives, and draw conclusions about everyday challenges to the best of their ability. In the new K–8 school, they will learn how to learn and be prepared for an undefined future.

What Kind of Skills Should Be Taught?

The range of skills that might be found in a K–8 curriculum is broad. Basic skills, such as the ability to read and write, learning to use the four operations in math, understanding basic scientific concepts and principles, and using new technologies, would dominate the early years.

There would also be taxonomic thinking (Bloom, 1984) that would teach the skills of recalling information, understanding and explaining information, using or applying information, analyzing information, assessing the worth of information, and generating new information.

Numerous thinking skills would also be infused throughout the content curriculum. The skill of asking good questions (inquiry), for instance, might be comprised of defining issues, gathering information, proposing alternatives, making judgments, and the consideration of issues of right and wrong.

Skills of social interaction would be taught throughout the K–8 curriculum. Examples of these skills would include accepting responsibility, respecting others, building relationships, making group decisions, and resolving conflicts.

Individual students would also learn a series of self-management skills for later life including things such as time management, establishing an identity, being organized, and seeing tasks through to their conclusion.

On an everyday basis, students would learn and use skills to treat subject matter content. The types of treatment that will assist students in developing the meaning of valued information include

- making comparisons,
- discovering parts,
- challenging ideas,
- guessing at solutions,
- troubleshooting,
- examining arguments,
- determining priorities, and
- assessing opposite views.

Sample Tasks for Each Learner

The personal development of each learner will involve a number of key areas that can be taught and learned while in school. These areas include self-management, the ability to interact socially, developing ethical character, and gaining a time perspective.

Becoming in charge of one's own behavior might mean

- being able to organize things,
- being able to manage time,
- choosing a healthy lifestyle,
- adopting safe behaviors, and
- establishing a positive identity.

Becoming capable of interacting socially might mean

- being able to work with others,
- accepting responsibility,
- being cooperative,
- respecting the rights of others, and
- being able to resolve conflicts.

Becoming ethical in character might mean

- understanding fundamental social values,
- showing concern for others,

- becoming empathetic, and
- acting in an ethical manner.

Gaining a time perspective might mean

- developing a world view,
- holding a sense of historical perspective,
- understanding the value of collective goals, and
- being concerned for future generations.

These lessons of living are easily taught in school by emphasizing skills and social experience as we conduct study in the traditional school subjects. Said another way, the manner in which the K–8 curriculum is taught will determine its meaning for students. By taking foundational learning and providing thinking skills and collaborative learning experiences, we can transition the K–8 curriculum from a set of measured and tested content standards to a more seamless learning pathway composed of generic learning skills. As one K–8 school in Northern California proposes in a new curriculum emphasis in their school mission statement,

> Our mission is to develop well-rounded students who are academically prepared, intellectually curious, adept at critical thinking, and possess problem-solving skills. It is our goal to prepare our students now, in high school and beyond, through the development of higher-order reasoning abilities.

Early studies in such a curriculum (Grades K–1) would be organized around investigation and interests of the learner. Large and generic concepts (big ideas) of the content areas can be introduced in simple form (Bruner, 1962). The seed pod placed in the Styrofoam cup in kindergarten windowsill, for example, represents the idea that certain conditions are needed for life. The trip to the fire station in the second grade represents the larger world of social services, and so forth.

Foundational studies (Grades 2–5) would be a broad and general education providing the student with subject knowledge, learning skills, and social experiences thought essential by educators. Because students will not progress uniformly through this material, opportunities for in-depth inquiry should be provided at this stage. Each student will master as much of the prescribed core of knowledge as possible.

As the student emerges with a strong foundational knowledge and a set of critical learning skills, the curriculum (Grades 6–7) can become livelier as areas of interest are explored and knowledge and skills extended.

The integration of subject areas (interdisciplinary) can become more pronounced, and the complexity and value dilemmas of an adult world introduced and studied.

Also, the concept of a *minimum–maximum curriculum* can be used in these years so that learning time is allocated to the most important needs. If necessary in this period, the curriculum may be unbalanced for some students so that an acceptable level of basic literacy is achieved while in the K–8 school. This focus on the "basics" is necessary and justifiable.

Finally, in the eighth grade, action learning would dominate the field of study as students learn practical applications of their general education. Higher uses of technology, service learning in the community, and studies of work would approximate the concerns of these near adolescents. Content specialization could be offered to some students in this year as part of a transitional eighth-grade program.

Collaborative Emphasis

In the real world, learning is almost always a collaborative process. Democratic problem solving, the new 24-hour work patterns of global businesses, and even family communication across vast distances require collaboration. When collaborative structures are combined with purposeful strategies for thinking, a powerful learning environment can be created.

The early work of cooperative learning advocates, plus later research on thinking styles, presents K–8 school planners with a number of useful techniques that can be built-in to any classroom instruction. These methodologies establish a new relationship between the teacher and student and place students at the center of the learning activity:

Jigsaw

Students on teams become experts on different parts of a problem and then teach each other what they have learned. As a group, they put the pieces of the puzzle together.

Add-On

Students sit at a round table and one student writes observations about an event. The paper is circulated, and each student adds to the observations using a different colored pencil to demonstrate participation. A discussion follows.

Think-Pair-Share

Partners in cooperative inquiry work independently to answer a question or solve a problem and then discuss their orientation with a partner. Together, the team shares their blended response.

Listen and Switch

In this timed activity, two or more students think out loud about a problem or issue while the partners listen and record. Then, at a signal, the roles are reversed, but the new leader must repeat the previous speaker's line of thought before beginning on their own.

Analyzing Debates

Different theories are proposed and analyzed by separate cooperative groups. The groups advocate for their theory as persuasively as possible. A large group discussion follows when all groups have presented their special theory case.

These techniques, and others found in the cooperative learning literature, can be conducted online as well as in the classroom. Student homework can include study partners who critique work or ideas using any of the patterns above. Parents can become partners in such Internet inquiry in the upper grades using search skills to find special knowledge for identified problems and issues.

Content knowledge → Treated by learning skills → Using collaboration
= Seamless learning for all

A Final Word About Content

Subject matter, or disciplines of study, contains common processes, key understandings, and big ideas that provide a perspective on life's experience. The artist, the mathematician, and the scientist would all notice different things in looking at an identical scene. Among the perspectives taught in school are historical, scientific, artistic, technological, communication, and mathematical. These are powerful tools for continued learning beyond the school years.

Subjects in school establish these perspectives by leading students through a body of prescribed knowledge and procedures that represent a discipline perspective. This information is usually a collection of the best thinking mankind has achieved in the given area. Accompanying this subject information are activating skills or ways of working that connect such learning to the real world. An example would be the deliberate process, taught as the scientific method, that all students learn in school. Another might be map skills to understand geography.

The subject disciplines are generally useful to all citizens as a way of thinking about the world in which we live. They also form a kind of common denominator among future citizens for discussing problems and issues. The imprint of these essentials is very impressive—for example, the way all Americans automatically visualize the United States of America at the center of any world map. Unlike the 9–12 secondary school, which emphasizes a mastery of content in all subjects (college preparation), the K–8 school can select the big ideas and skills that characterize each subject area. Students would receive an orientation, foundational material, expansion, and application practice in each subject as they progress through the K–8 school curriculum. The various skills of learning, applicable to all students at all levels in all subjects, would always form the common denominator of the curriculum.

QUESTIONS FOR STUDY GROUPS

1. How does the life-skills emphasis suggested by the author avoid the traditional arguments about academic rigor in the intermediate curriculum?

2. What is meant by a minimum–maximum curriculum during Grades 6 and 7?

3. How can the skills of collaboration best be taught at the various levels of the K–8 curriculum?

4. What must parents know to understand this new K–8 curriculum?

5. How is this suggested curriculum a departure from past curriculum designs?

SUMMARY

The new K–8 school can create a useful and seamless curriculum by focusing on general outcomes of education, rather than solely on academic content or testing. The traditional purpose of K–8 schooling is general education: providing all students lessons as preparation for living after school. These life skills, desired for all students, are the basis for defining the K–8 curriculum.

The K–8 curriculum should be organized into four levels, reflecting the developmental stages of students from age 5–13. These stages are orientation, mastery of foundational material, exploration and expansion, and applications of the curriculum.

Many lists of outcomes exist, but most modern lists suggest skills and behaviors for 21st century living. At the conclusion of the eighth grade, for example, students should be in charge of their own behaviors, be capable of social interaction, possess an ethical character, and see their own existence in a time perspective. Each school will want to prioritize its own list of the most important outcomes.

Teaching throughout the K–8 curriculum should be characterized by collaborative experiences. Specific skills for interacting with others can be taught at any level and in all content areas.

REFERENCES

Bloom, B. (1984). *Taxonomy of educational objectives.* Boston: Allyn and Bacon.

Bruner, J. (1962). *The process of education.* Cambridge: Harvard University Press.

Freestone, M. (2006, September). *Thinking for understanding.* Minneapolis: DesignShare.

Partnership for 21st Century Skills. (2008). *Policy Recommendations for Preparing America for the Global Skills Race.* Available from Partnership for 21st Century Skills, 177 North Church Avenue, Tucson, AZ.

Instructional Patterns for the New K–8 School

Educators in Grades K–8 believe that the student is the critical player in learning because it is the student who interprets what is taught based on his or her background. Said another way, how the student "treats" or interacts with any lesson determines its meaning to that student. Educators at this level also believe that the learning medium is important in influencing the students' perception of what is taught in school. Lectures, small group work, and computer-assisted instruction will have a different effect on the very same subject matter lesson. For these reasons, the instructional pattern established in the new K–8 school is of utmost importance to the kind of learning students will experience.

To be effective, the new K–8 school must feature a novel instructional design: unique organizational patterns for each developmental level, new assumptions about learner capacities, new applied methods, new tools for student assessment, and new arrangements for involving parents as learning partners. The K–8 school, through these new patterns, seeks to be both more personal and intellectually challenging as an educational experience for students. Creating a balance between these outcomes will be a challenge for all K–8 leaders (Davis 2008).

GENERAL DESIGN

The general design for learning, suggested by the author, attempts to match instructional patterns to the developmental level of the students.

The youngest students (K–1) are absorbing new information in a new environment. The students are to learn simple concepts and basic skills while being introduced to activities that will build up their background and experience. A single teacher, or perhaps a pair of teachers, will provide a safe and caring environment for this beginning.

In Grades 2–5 (ages 7–10), students will use those early experiences and preliminary skills (reading, writing, computation) to learn core foundational subject matter and skills prescribed by state standards. Students will learn with several teachers and with the aid of computer-based instruction. The goal will be for each student to attain a platform of knowledge and skills at the minimal level as identified by state laws.

In Grades 6–7 (ages 11–12), most students will be ready to experience more in-depth learning and explore applications of subject matter. Students may also want to develop personal interests and talents via short courses. Some students will still be mastering foundational material and the minimum–maximum instructional design will allow schools to "unbalance" the curriculum to provide these needy students with additional time to master basics. On the other end of the learning continuum, students who can benefit from advanced academic study will find opportunities to do so.

In the sixth and seventh grades, students will work in learning communities, experience interdisciplinary work, and use technology to expand horizons and interests, a fitting emphasis for this developmental stage. This will be a period of major intellectual growth and capacity. All students, however, will master a guaranteed level of basic literacy.

Finally, in the eighth grade (ages 13+), students will apply the knowledge and skills they have mastered to the community and beyond. Regardless of the degree of content mastery, each student will possess a set of thinking skills that will allow them to engage problems and issues in adulthood.

Eighth graders will simulate citizenship through service learning and very practical applications of the curriculum, such as learning how to file taxes, conduct comparison shopping, job seeking, and studying common family living problems.

ORGANIZATION PATTERNS

The traditional elementary school has featured self-contained classroom instruction for nearly 100 years. In the early grades, a single teacher acts as a parental figure in teaching the students the entire curriculum. In the upper grades of the elementary school, several teachers may interact with the students for content specialization, but the majority of student time

Figure 4.1   The general instructional design for K–8 education

K–1	Students are introduced to schooling, basic learning skills, and early experiences to build up background.	Students will be with a single teacher or a pair of teachers. A safe and caring learning environment is provided.
2–5	Students are mastering basic foundational knowledge and skills that are prescribed by state learning standards. Each student will exit with big ideas and skills for future learning.	Students in 2–5 will spend most time in self-contained classrooms with a teacher or a team of teachers who rotate students for instruction in math, science, language arts, and social studies.
6–7	Students at this level will explore uses of the skills and knowledge they have mastered. Personal interests can be addressed and talents uncovered. A minimum–maximum curriculum will act to guarantee achievement.	Most students will be instructed by teaching teams and experience a wide variety of short-courses and self-guided study. The Internet will provide options for some students. Students needing more time to master the foundational areas will divide their time accordingly between basics and exploration.
8	In the eighth grade students will apply school learning in a variety of settings (school, community) and in adult problem solving and community service.	Learning communities and action research teams will structure learning experiences for students in school and beyond. Each student will practice the application of thinking skills in practical everyday areas.

is spent with "their" teacher. Most elementary schools have a warm and personal atmosphere for students.

Middle schools, by contrast, have used teams of teachers to teach the many subjects to a single group or "team" of students. Such specialization has been effective in providing content specialization to a wide range of students, but in some schools the personal contact between teacher and student has been diminished.

The K–8 school will be most effective in teaching all students when it blends these two approaches to classroom organization. Because of the general instructional design, the organization of the K–8 school may appear distinctive at various levels. The students new to the school (K–1) will experience a blend of activity learning and regular whole classroom study. In Grades 2–5, student study will be more formal, in classrooms, and focused on the kind of outcomes that state standards have required. In Grades 6–7, instruction will be more flexible and feature many teacher–student combinations, as well as applied computer-based instruction. In the Grade 8, the walls between schooling and the real world will begin to fade away as students conduct problem solving and service learning in the school and in the community.

It will be the goal of the new K–8 school that each student who exits the curriculum will be literate, skilled at continuous learning, knowledgeable about global issues, future oriented, and prepared for general adult living. State learning standards will measure traditional achievement, while a portfolio of experiences, skill lists, and work products will measure individual student accomplishments.

Figure 4.2   Classroom organization

K–1	Self-contained and community-based instruction (field trips)
2–5	Self-contained with possibility of teachers paired for content specialization
6–7	Teaching teams with parental supplement and considerable computer-assisted instruction
8	Learning communities, self-contained and community-based instruction, computer-based instruction

Continuing the tradition of developmentally appropriate curricula, the new K–8 school would view student growth and development as occurring in four distinct stages: early childhood, later childhood, preadolescence, and adolescence. Each student would be perceived as a unique individual, having his or her own rate of growth through these predictable stages of development. A continuum of student progress would be defined by mastery of learning (thinking) skills, as well as the mastery of prescribed content as measured by state standards and testing for various grade levels.

MODIFYING STANDARDS-BASED CURRICULUM

Standards-based curricula, and their companion testing programs, measure student progress against learning targets established by state law. Such judgments, mixing criterion-referenced evaluation with norm-referenced evaluation, often discourage students and create instructional problems for teachers. Ten instructional practices can be used to encourage the success of each individual student within a standards-based curriculum, regardless of their rate of progress, in the new K–8 school.

1. Acceptance of Multiple Intelligences

Studies of effective leadership in industry suggest that leaders of the future will need to possess not only well-developed intellectual abilities, but also equally impressive social and emotional skills. Until recently, educators have focused primarily on only two types of intelligence, logical and linguistic, with almost no attention to other kinds of performance. Under standards-based education, this focus has been even more narrowly ordered. Accepting that there is more to intelligence than "school smarts" is a first step in modifying the standards-based classroom to serve the K–8 student.

The development of practical intelligence is highly relevant to adaptation, shaping, and selection in everyday life. Traditional theories of intelligence hold that intelligence is a goal-directed mental activity, characterized by efficient problem solving, critical thinking, and effective abstract reasoning. Sternberg, in speaking of emotional intelligence (Sternberg, 2008), defines human intelligence as "the mental abilities necessary for adaptation, as well as shaping and selecting, any environment." Noncognitive intelligence, including intrapersonal and interpersonal skills, may be as important to the future lives of students as the traditional skills and knowledge taught in schools each day. Some research studies suggest that up to 80% of a person's success in life is determined by their emotional intelligence or "street smarts" (Goleman, 2005).

An example of such relevant and substantial research can be drawn from the Somerville Study, a forty-year longitudinal study of 450 boys who grew up in Somerville, Massachusetts. According to this study, conventional IQ had little to do with the success they experienced in life. What made the biggest difference were the abilities developed during the early years such as being able to handle frustration, control emotions, and get along with other people (Cherniss, 2000). Another study, of 300 top-level executives from fifteen global companies, found that six emotional competencies distinguished the "stars" from the average executive: influence, team leadership, organizational awareness, self-confidence, achievement drive, and leadership. Many other studies have shown that failure in leadership (derailment below expectation) is frequently attributed to the lack of interpersonal and intrapersonal skills of the leader.

Leaders in K–8 schools should become familiar with these and other studies that suggest that simple knowledge is no longer the only critical element for adult living. Leaders must intercede to help teachers set up an environment that consists of adult nurturing, healthy peer relationships, and sensitive and responsive support service. These climate factors in a K–8 school mediate between the academic requirements and the motivation of students to use knowledge and apply skills beyond schooling. Students need greater opportunities to problem solve with others and to examine what has worked and what has not worked in such collaborations. Students need more opportunity for introspection as they master predetermined outcomes that are tested in schools. Such opportunities are featured in this prescribed curriculum for the new K–8 school.

The acceptance of multiple intelligences is also the keystone to the acceptance of diversity in school and in our world. It is not difficult to argue that the increasingly global nature of business, the growing reliance of technology, international communications, and the cooperation needed to complete global projects call for future citizens who are capable of interacting, contemplating, and relearning. Figure 4.3 displays nine possible types of human intelligences as proposed by Howard Gardner of Harvard University (Gardner, 1999).

Figure 4.3   Nine intelligences found in schools

Linguistic intelligence	Capacity to use language to express what's on your mind and to understand others
Logical/mathematical intelligence	Capacity to understand the underlying principles of systems, and manipulate numbers and quantities
Musical/rhythmic intelligence	Capacity to think in music, hearing and manipulating patterns
Bodily/kinesthetic intelligence	Capacity to use the body to solve problems and demonstrate ideas
Spatial intelligence	Ability to represent the spatial world through mental activities
Naturalist intelligence	Demonstrated sensitivity to the natural world and insightful to natural relationships
Intrapersonal intelligence	Understanding of self and reacting to the environment using this capacity
Interpersonal intelligence	Ability to understand others and interact accordingly
Existential intelligence	Ability to pose and ponder questions about ultimate realities

Source: Jon Wiles (2005), *Curriculum Essentials.* Adapted from the works of Howard Gardner.

2. Using Learning Styles

Knowing about learning styles can help teachers become more sensitive to the differences students bring to the classroom. Such knowledge can also contribute to the design of meaningful learning experiences that meet students' learning preferences. Finally, knowing about learning styles can help teachers address the needs of poorly prepared students, those who most often drop out of school after the eighth grade and perform poorly on standardized tests.

Three types of *style dominance* found in the literature include visual dominance, auditory dominance, and spatial dominance. Visual learners receive knowledge through a broad visual screen, which can include teacher body language and facial expression. Displays and illustrations, handouts, and multimedia sources such as the computer are preferred. Auditory learners do best in verbal lectures, discussions, and hearing what others say. The tone, pitch, and speed of the input are very important to understanding. Tactile learners learn best by doing, with hands-on exercises and interaction with the world around them. Such learners crave activity and movement. All of these learning styles are present in K–8 school learners and at all four levels.

Futurists tell us that we presently have 100% more new information in our lives about every 5 years. Teachers cannot continue to base their practice on simply imparting information, but instead must help each student learn how to learn. Making learning natural, according to student strengths not weaknesses, will help students become lifelong learners in our changing world. Some students, for instance, prefer their learning "concrete" or direct to their senses. Other students, who favor abstraction, like to conceive ideas and use intuition, looking beyond what appears to be present. For some students, information may best be received in a linear, piece-by-piece manner. Other students would prefer knowledge to be delivered in chunks or in a conceptual format. The growth and development of each individual student predetermines much of that student's learning capacity at various stages of development.

The bottom line on learning styles is that when there is a mismatch between the student learning style and the teacher's methodology, bad things happen. Students may become bored and listless, agitated, perform poorly on tests, get discouraged about the curriculum and their own capacity, become hostile or unresponsive, and even just drop out. A curriculum, even one teaching to a standards-based format, can be varied in its presentation format and serve all students.

3. Curriculum Differentiation

Curriculum differentiation is a broad idea that addresses the need to tailor the classroom environment and the instructional practices to create a unique learning experience for each child. This might include things like deleting already-mastered material from the curriculum, adding content or skill practice to the existing curriculum, extending enrichment activities, allowing for early entry into study areas, writing instructional units for groups of students with like needs, and providing a minimum–maximum option in later grades. Altering the environment, changing the process of learning, modifying the content, and tailoring evaluation products all would be considered differentiation.

The logic of differentiation can best be understood in terms of the range of learning in a single classroom. A typical seventh grade classroom would have some near nonreaders and some near college-level readers. A differentiated classroom seeks to tap into the readiness levels, interests, and learning profile of each student with the goal of maximizing individual achievement. This is a quite different strategy than one that insists that all students master minimal-level standards, at grade level, and evidence them on a standardized test.

Tomlinson (Tomlinson, 1999) sees four things that characterize a differentiated classroom.

1. Instruction is introduced at the conceptual level with multiple avenues to mastery

2. Assessment is flexible and found within the curriculum

3. Grouping is flexible and changes as tasks change

4. Students are active participants in the learning process

Instruction would be characterized by abstraction, complexity, variety, and flexibility. In the classroom one might see multilevel texts, learning contracts, group investigation, Internet usage, and interest centers. The observer would also see significant collaborative learning in the differentiated classroom.

The reader may be wondering if there is a basic conflict between this type of teaching and learning and the traditional standards-based classroom. There doesn't have to be any compromise between these two designs. Most standards are not finite points to be mastered, but consist of knowledge and skills, such as factual material or problem-solving processes, that are to be demonstrated. These are standards that can be demonstrated and tested at many levels of competence, and therefore can be learned at many levels of abstraction. We simply have no evidence that treating all students alike promotes achievement or standards mastery. The differentiated classroom is a learning strategy to accomplish the same ends as those identified in standards-based instruction.

4. Cooperative Learning

Interacting with others, cooperatively, is an obvious skill needed in the 21st century. Work, communication, travel, and education all demand various forms of cooperation. The cooperative learning methodology found in schools since the 1980s is an invaluable tool in the age of standards-based education. As a method, cooperative learning is a carefully structured procedure in which students are held accountable for individual contribution to a group project. Various cooperative learning designs teach that the group as a whole can be stronger than individual members. Positive interdependence is structured by having mutual goals, shared resources, and assigned roles.

Examples of skills taught through cooperative projects would be joint planning, decision making, deferring judgment, consensus building, listening, formulating good questions, learning to ask for help or give assistance, giving and receiving directions, and sharing materials. All of these, and more, are found in the everyday work world and are being prescribed by prestigious study groups.

Supplementing intellectual growth with both social and personal development pays long-term dividends in knowledge use. Group assignments, for instance, help students combine prior knowledge with new knowledge, and re-form knowledge based on new input. The various common models of cooperative learning, such as jigsaw, group investigation, think-pair-share, or teams-and-games, allow for individual student learning styles to be integrated into the classroom. Research by Robert Slavin indicates that simply grouping the middle-level classes and the upper-level classes of students will produce achievement as high as that achieved by the upper-level students alone (Slavin, 2008).

5. Interdisciplinary Learning

Interdisciplinary learning, sometimes called integrated study, occurs when students explore knowledge as related to certain aspects of their environment. Cutting across traditional subject areas, and organized around real-life themes, the curriculum is brought into meaningful association with broad goals of education. Such content-rich and skill-rich curricula develop a learner's power to create new models, systems, and structures. Interdisciplinary instruction mimics real life and prepares students for lifelong learning.

This method has been used in many middle schools for years, and that experience can serve as the basis for schoolwide applications using interdisciplinary units.

6. Problem-Based Learning

Increasingly, all schools are moving the curriculum toward an application of knowledge using a problems-based format. Known to teachers as *problems-based learning,* or PBL, these curriculums purposefully create scenarios and structured problems based on desired curriculum outcomes (skills, knowledge). The student is led to actively define problems and construct potential solutions using things learned in school.

Being an effective problem solver is a goal of almost every standards-based document (SCANS for example), and most school goal statements suggest the need for critical thinking and problem-solving skills. Being an effective problem solver in the new information age has become a primary goal of education.

Students working in PBL learn to clearly define problems, develop alternative hypotheses, access and evaluate data, alter hypotheses to accommodate new data, develop solutions that specifically fit problems and so forth. The Internet is a perfect connecter for problems and the information that can serve as a solution to those problems. PBL can be applied effectively in the local community. Imperfect problems, and the imperfect solutions sometimes developed by students using PBL, mirror the real world in which we live.

7. Mentoring

Mentoring programs come in all shapes and sizes, with the most common model being a helper assisting less-able learners in the elementary and middle schools. The idea of having an adult, or another older student, as a work partner in a problem-based curriculum has a lot of possibilities for K–8 schools. Such mentors can provide a time-perspective to tasks, as well as open the community to the school and its students.

The world outside of school operates much differently than the world inside school. Real-world problems and solutions often contain moral dilemmas calling for choices and compromise. The real world is more technological than the school world, and a lot more interdependent. Values sometimes define choices in the real world, and such values are many times the result of long-term experience. The real world is highly political as citizens compete for scarce resources.

Older students can become advocates for learning when working with younger students in a mentoring role. The credibility of the older student may be quite high in the eyes of the younger student.

Mentors who have undergone training are usually good listeners. They can dedicate time to helping students see relationships. They can also serve as extensions for the student into the outside adult population. Adult mentors are usually willing to share their life experiences and are sometimes open to learning new things themselves. Most mentors like young people and are volunteering their most valuable commodity, time.

8. Service Learning

New on the scene is something called *service learning,* which in another time might have been called *community work.* Service learning connects classroom learning to real-world experiences. It makes students more aware of their surroundings. The development of interpersonal skills through service learning projects can't be understated. Research suggests that service learning promotes fewer disciplinary referrals, higher trust of adults, and a greater acceptance of cultural diversity. Through service learning, students can experience empowerment.

There is significant evidence to suggest that students who participate in service learning activities show gains on achievement tests, in reading and basic skills, and earn higher grade point averages. Schools using service learning on a regular basis report higher attendance and stronger student motivation.

Finally, the impact on communities where service learning has become a part of the curriculum is positive. In these environments, students are perceived as part of the community, valued resources and contributing members. Parents and community members can see the curriculum and support school programming.

9. Flexible Block Schedules

The flexible block schedule addresses the concern for meeting the needs of individual students and the creative use of time in classrooms. By offering a choice of time configurations, these schedules enhance the work of teaching teams by providing for common planning time. They also allow teams of teachers to provide instruction to different size groups of students, and for flexible lengths of time. As noted earlier, the absence of state regulation in most states allows the length of a class period to be variable or fixed in blocks of time from ten minutes to all day (modular schedules). Research of the use of flexible schedules shows a contribution to cohesiveness in student groups, better attendance, and greater empowerment of teachers (Merebloom, 1996).

Because most middle schools have used block schedules or modified block schedules for thirty years, the practice can quickly be applied to the K–8 program.

10. Looping

Looping is a technique that allows a teacher or a team of teachers to stay with a group of students over time. Usually, teachers "loop" up with a class and therefore have a two-year period of contact with the students. This practice contributes to better use of instructional time and better social and personal relations (and less discipline problems) at the classroom level. Teachers also report better relationships with parents when they work with students for a longer period of time.

Looping has been found in both K–5 elementary schools and in some 6–8 middle schools. This sound practice, which personalizes the curriculum while promoting better achievement, can be easily applied to the four-tier K–8 school model.

Standards-based curriculum does not have to be only about scoring well in high stakes testing. K–8 leaders can take a fairly neutral state-mandated curriculum and activate it by designed instructional organization and the use of new and tested ways of working with teachers and students in the classroom. Accepting the value of multiple intelligences, learning styles, differentiated curriculum delivery, cooperative learning, interdisciplinary teaching, problem-based learning, mentoring, service learning, flexible schedules, and looping can all direct learning standards toward fuller utilization (see Figure 4.4).

Figure 4.4   Ten instructional practices to modify the new K–8 curriculum

Multiple intelligences

Learning styles

Differentiated instruction

Cooperative learning

Interdisciplinary teaching

Problem-based learning

Mentoring

Service learning

Flexible schedules

Looping

NEW USES FOR SCHOOL BUILDINGS

Although most new K–8 programs will be housed in former elementary structures, those traditional "cells and bells" facilities can be modified to support the instructional intent of the K–8 curriculum. General goals for any building would include a more relaxed learning environment, providing better opportunities for communication, bringing together the various disciplines of study into a focused whole, more effective uses of technology, and opening up access to the school to parents and the community.

Award-winning school design firms have used the following organizational patterns to characterize the new uses of the school facility.

1. Small learning communities

2. Learning studios

3. Welcoming entry

4. Life skills areas

5. Interior and exterior vistas

6. Soft seating

7. Casual eating areas

8. Collaborative spaces

9. Natural daylight

10. Connectivity with community

NEW DEPLOYMENT PATTERNS FOR TEACHERS

The assignment of teachers to work with students provides an opportunity to change how learning occurs in the new K–8 building. Self-contained classroom elementary teachers and team-based middle school teachers both have many roles. Both groups of teachers move effortlessly between regular academic roles and more interpersonal roles. This asset, to be found in every new K–8 building, allows teachers to define themselves as more than grade-level teachers, and more than a content specialist (see Figure 4.5).

The K–8 building can easily use teachers in two patterns that have been found effective in working with students. First, in Grades 2–7, teachers

Figure 4.5   Organization of teachers by tier

K–1	Self-contained, 2-year looping
2–5	Self-contained, two-teacher teaming for academic specialization
6–7	Teams of interdisciplinary teachers, looping, enrichment, and remediation
8	Self-contained, problem-based, and service learning

can be assigned nongraded or multiaged learning groups according to the tasks confronted and the attainment level of individual students. Having students from a number of grades working together in the new K–8 school will be facilitated by the skills-continuum orientation of the curriculum. Problem-based instruction and projects for enrichment are natural organizations for nongraded instruction.

A second technique of promise for the K–8 school is looping, a practice in which the teacher stays with a class of students for one or more years of instruction. This practice seems especially appropriate for the K–1 and 6–7 levels of the new K–8 school.

NEW WAYS OF ASSESSING STUDENTS

Students in the new K–8 school will be assessed in several ways during their attendance. States' standards testing, of course, will be attained at Grades 3, 5, and 8 in most states. Students will also be validated in the attainment of learning skills and thinking skills taught throughout the nine years. These assessments might monitor: (a) exposure, (b) application and use, or (c) learning products in physical or electronic portfolios.

Reporting to parents about the progress of each student is an opportunity for every new K–8 school to "break out" of the old report card procedures. Because most states do not require specific report card documentation before the ninth grade, these progress reports can be as formal or informal as the school desires. A preferred way to monitor student growth and communicate with parents about student progress would be via an electronic report card accessible online.

One school in Northern California is a leader in such a reporting system, as they regularly convey to parents whether a student is making grade-level progress in acquiring knowledge or mastering learning skills (Stockton Unified School District, 2008). Some areas of student behavior outside of academic performance are also reported. Students demonstrating grade-level competence receive a check with no further letter grade designations. Such a system could be complemented by student work-samples available for viewing online.

NEW PATTERNS FOR INVOLVING PARENTS IN INSTRUCTION

One of the driving forces behind the K–8 movement is the desire by parents to remain close to their child's school through the eighth grade. The design of the new K–8 school allows parents many new roles on a daily basis. In Grades K–1 the parent can be involved in the extensive field trips and orientation activities. In Grades 2–5, parents can be involved in the mastery of fundamentals by receiving e-mail attachments describing what is happening in the classroom and homework (attachments) for parents and students to work on together. In Grades 6–7, parents can join the school to model occupational possibilities for students and to help them explore new areas of interest.

Finally, in the eighth grade, parents can help organize problem-based learning and service learning opportunities in the community.

The new K–8 school should recognize the frustration of parents in being shut out of junior high schools and middle schools. They are forceful in their desire to see their child's school as a true community school. These parents represent a rich supplement to the school's instructional staff. After all, parents were every student's first teacher.

QUESTIONS FOR STUDY GROUPS

1. What are five ways that parents can become more involved in K–8 school activities?

2. What problems, if any, might occur from having different organizational patterns at different grade levels in the same building?

3. How do the new assumptions about students differ from our traditional assumptions at the elementary school level?

4. What might a schedule look like in a new K–8 school as outlined by the author?

SUMMARY

Instruction in the new K–8 school will require change in order to meet the goal of serving all students. The curriculum of the school will reflect the developmental stage of the students, thinking skills will serve as the common denominator for all learning, and ten methodologies will be applied in order to make the school more open and personal.

In addition, the new K–8 school will use existing buildings in new ways, deploy the teaching staff in a different manner, use novel ways of assessing students and reporting progress, and involve parents in the school to a greater degree than ever before.

REFERENCES

Cherniss, C. (2000). *Emotional intelligence: What it is and why it matters.* Presented at the Society of Industrial and Organizational Psychology in New Orleans, at the Consortium for Research on Emotional Intelligence in Organizations.

Davis, G. (2008). *Turning points: Educating adolescents in the 21st century* (Carnegie Council on Adolescent Development). New York: Carnegie Corporation.

Gardner, H. (1999). *Intelligence reframed.* New York: Basic Books.

Goleman, D. (1995). *Emotional intelligence: Why it can matter more than IQ.* New York: Bantam.

Merebloom, E. (Ed.). (1996). *Research summary # 2: Flexible scheduling.* Westerville, OH: National Middle School Association.

Slavin, R. (2008). *Educational psychology: Theory and practice.* Boston: Allyn & Bacon.

Sternberg, R. (2008). *Cognitive psychology.* Belmont, CA: Wadsworth.

Stockton Unified School District. (2008). *General K–8 report card information and forms.* Retrieved February 22, 2009, from http://www.stockton.k12.ca.us/html/k8reportcard.html

Tomlinson, C. (1999). *The differentiated classroom: Responding to the needs of all learners.* Alexandria, VA: Association for Supervision and Curriculum Development.

A Return on Investment

The prescription for curriculum development in the new K–8 school, as presented in this book, is extensive. In combining the best of the traditional elementary program with the best of middle school programs, there will be changes made everywhere. The grade-level organization, the curriculum, staff development, the deployment of teachers, the organization of learning, the assessment of students, and many other critical ingredients for operating a school will be changing. The new American K–8 will be the first true 21st century school.

In this chapter the reader will find descriptions of how the school might look to the various stakeholders: parents, students, teachers, and administrators. Although it is acknowledged that no two K–8 schools will ever be the same, every school that is planning or operating a K–8 program should find ideas in this chapter that are useful.

PARENTS

Parents in small towns, the suburbs, and city school districts are demanding a school much like the one projected in this book. Parents want smallness, they want their child known by teachers, and they want a school that benefits all students during the entire nine years of attendance. Parents may not know all the words that educators use to describe school philosophies and preferences, but it is clear they want a safe, caring, and productive experience for their child. What parent wouldn't want these things? Intuitively, all parents recognize the importance of school for their child's life.

According to the United States Department of Education, only 68% of American students will complete high school, one half of those graduates will attend some sort of college, and just one quarter of those who go to college make it to their sophomore year (Brumfield, 2005). These are alarming statistics, even worse in some urban and rural areas, reflecting something terribly wrong with the way our schools prepare students for the future. We must stop "saving the best and shooting the rest" during the K–8 grades. An opportunity to change this dreadful pattern is at hand throughout America. The new K–8 school, unquestionably, is about "general education" for the vast majority of students in attendance. And, for almost one-fourth of the K–8 pupils, this school will be the finishing school; the last stop before adult citizenship in our society.

Parents understand all too well that today's schools are not designed for 21st century workforce skills or the critical learning skills needed to succeed academically beyond high school. Students need to learn organizational techniques, social skills, problem-solving approaches, and ethics in addition to the traditional knowledge foundations held by all educated people (Core Knowledge Foundation, 2005). Many parents understand the connection between educational attainment and socioeconomic level. They want their children to be educated and successful in life beyond school.

Few schools recognize the power of the parent in terms of school achievement. Early in life they contribute greatly to their child's neurodevelopment, including attention, memory, language, understanding relationships, sequencing, and basic motor skills. Once the child is in school, the degree of goal-setting and planning a parent does with the student directly influences academic success. Some researchers have gone so far as to make the thought-provoking statement that the parent and the home have as much influence on academic success as the teacher in the school (Greenwood, 1993).

In his fascinating book, *The Other Parent* (Steyer, 2002), James Steyer documents how parents and their children have been separated by the new media. "Roaming among TVs, VCRs, the Internet, radios, CD players, movie screens, and electronic games, kids can easily spend more time in this vast mediascape than in the real world," reports Steyer. By this author's estimate, based on various studies, kids today spend 40% less time with their parents than in the 1960s.

Parents are demanding greater involvement in school activities, and parent involvement in the curriculum of any new K–8 school can be unprecedented. The elementary school, of course, has always welcomed parents as teacher assistants, field trip chaperones and room mothers and fathers. It is expected that in the first tier of the new K–8 school, such participation would certainly continue. Such participation has always paid dividends for students, teachers, and schools.

One distinctly different kind of contact that can be established by any K–8 school today is communicating directly with parents via e-mail. As of November, 2007, 71.5% of the American population has been penetrated by the Internet (highest in the world). That percentage may be even higher for the subpopulation of homes with children in school (Internet World Status, 2008). There is no longer any reason for parents to not be up to speed with what is happening in their child's classroom. The Internet can be the parent's window on the classroom, and the school's conduit to the home.

Software, currently in use in public schools, demonstrates how thoroughly parents can be involved in their child's education. Parents can access homework, tests, grades, current progress in each class, and important messages from teachers and administrators. In return, parents can post important messages for the teacher or administrator and make requests of the school (eSIS Parent Assistant, n.d.).

In the second tier of the curriculum, Grades 2–5, students are studying foundational material and mastering basic learning skills in fairly traditional classroom settings. The K–8 goal for all students would be to leave this level of education as completely literate and achieving learners. The role of parents in assisting students could be greatly expanded in Grades 2–5, utilizing the spirit of Japanese education, which sees the parent as a full learning partner. An airtight homework connection with parents is the key to such cooperation.

In the third tier of study, students in the K–8 school are experiencing significant growth in their intellectual abilities (cognitive reasoning). In addition, their interests and their talents emerge and expand greatly during these years. The curriculum design of this level is meant to enlarge intellectual horizons through inquiry and exploration of social issues, subjects, and work-related opportunities. For students still mastering the basics (minimum–maximum curriculum), additional time will be spent in small group study or individualized mentoring.

Parents can serve this level of study in many ways. For students needing additional assistance, parents might serve as learning mentors. For students who are opening new intellectual territories, parents might provide insight to the world of work or hobbies that have intellectual qualities (astronomy, ham radio). The "corridor curriculum" found in some middle schools allows students to visit stations manned by parents during school hours that are focused on occupational destinations. Parents might also assist the school in providing leadership in the organization of out-of-school learning opportunities.

Finally, in the fourth tier (eighth grade only), parents might become part of service learning teams, helping link the school to community service clubs and projects. Parents might also help enrich academic extension by providing real-world access to societal problems and work. Apprenticeships are also a possibility for some students.

Parents are adamant, this time around, that they won't be excluded from the schooling process. They favor school achievement, but they also want their child engaged in successful and supportive learning experiences. Parents want to be involved in their child's school, and they must be if all students are to succeed (see Figure 5.1).

Figure 5.1 Parent experiences in the K–8 school

Tier 1	PreK skill development participant
	Teacher assistants
	Field trip chaperones
	Room parent
	Internet monitor of student achievement
Tier 2	Homework partner
	Internet monitor of student achievement
Tier 3	Learning mentor
	Intellectual hobbies
	Corridor curriculum for occupational projections
	Organizing out-of-school learning activities
Tier 4	Service learning team member
	School link to community organizations
	Apprenticeships for academic extension

STUDENTS

Students enter the K–8 school in kindergarten with varied backgrounds. In today's complex economy, with both parents working, nearly 80% of these students will have already experienced some institutional school-like experience before attending the K–8 school. Some students will have already been taught early reading and math skills by parents or preschool. To a large degree, the "school intelligence" of these entering pupils will depend on their prior experience: reference points, communication skills, self-control, and general happiness. These school traits are also the result of the quality of their home life and parental support at home. The new K–8 school must take these students as they find them and provide the students a thorough general education in nine short years.

K–8 schools have the opportunity to connect with parents before the student comes to school. To the degree that the curriculum of the K–8 school is clear, parents and preK experiences can reinforce school readiness. The initiation of such school contact with parents and community rests with the K–8 leader.

The tasks of educating in the first 2 years of schooling (K–1) include a social orientation, providing conceptual experiences, teaching the foundations of basic literacy, screening the individual student for any learning challenges, and assisting the students in large motor development through planned physical activity.

Particularly important to later study, in the upper levels of curriculum in the K–8 school, is to provide early (Grades K–1) experiences that will establish a conceptual base for advanced learning. When children take field trips, for example, the school is establishing reference points for later teaching and also introducing the students to a prediscipline (subject matter) field of knowledge. By the conclusion of first grade, through trips to fire stations, art galleries, electric plants, and plays, the school is helping the student to "map" their surroundings. Visits by poets, policemen, sports stars, plumbers, and other occupational role models help the students to define themselves. When the curriculum moves into strong subject matter foundations in the second grade, all students will have these common reference points about life beyond school.

Another important experience for later learning in the K–8 school will be the socialization skills learned through working together, play, and rule setting. Getting along with others, especially others different from ourselves, is a crucial 21st century skill. Play at this stage of development, in school, is appropriate and essential school learning.

Finally, in K–1, it is mandatory that all learning follow a solid introduction that builds basic skills. These basics would include preparation for reading, writing, and computational skills, and also early technology skills. Most five- and six-year-olds are completely capable of using computers, and many do so at home after school is out.

In the second through the fifth grade, students in the new K–8 school will be mastering foundational information and skills that will be useful for the duration of their lifetime. Whereas much of the instruction will be structured, mentors and technology can be used at this level for drill and practice. What is desired for all students by the end of the fifth grade is that they possess a strong core of knowledge in subject areas and also have the individual learning skills and technological skills to become a self-sustaining learner. Students who need more time to accomplish these basics may carry over their work into the minimum–maximum curriculum of Grades 6–7. By including this curriculum option, all students have up to six years of schooling to learn to read, write, compute, and possess basic computer skills. Subject matter mastery in these grades can and should be assessed by standardized state testing programs.

The parents of each child can assist the school in meeting these targets set by learning standards and testing in nearly all states. Routines for home study can be established, with school help, and teachers and students can use e-mail to exchange information about student assignments and progress (homework assignments can be attached to e-mail). It is important that assessment of student progress be highly specific at this tier, indicating student progress in terms of identified skill mastery and tested achievement. For many students, this will be the one time in their schooling experience where basic literacy is expected and achieved.

There will, of course, be other kinds of learning at this stage of development. Basic physical development, sex role identification, social development, occupational projection, and a host of other developmental tasks are being mastered by students from ages seven to eleven. Other socializing agencies, such as scouting and organized sports programs, will also contribute to the growth of students during this tier of study.

In the sixth and seventh grades, the new K–8 school will find a widening range of student achievement and development. Some students will begin to fall behind and become discouraged with school as they search for competence. Others will have completed the core literacy and knowledge section of the curriculum and will be ready for advanced academic challenges. The K–8 program offers all patterns of development a viable education through three organizational mediums. First, the students will be placed on *family teams* in which a group of teachers can address their needs as individuals. Many students become disengaged from school at this age, and an adult who knows them personally is extremely important to the student. Knowing the students well will also help the school avoid the harmful practice of static ability grouping.

The second organizational response or medium is the minimum–maximum curriculum feature. Schools will be keeping electronic profiles of student achievement through these years. Students who are seriously behind in basic skill development or knowledge acquisition can spend a greater proportion of their academic school day (their redefined school day) devoting time to these things in sixth and seventh grade. An unbalanced program of studies, emphasizing basic skills, is appropriate at this point in the program. There are opportunities for peers and older students to help tutor those needing assistance during these years.

The teams of sixth and seventh grade teachers can divide their students in a number of learning configurations or groupings. For example, 4 teachers in a team with 100 students could form 4 groups of 25, or groups of 30, 30, 30, and 10, or even 40, 40, 10, 10 (large–small group activity). Through such cooperative planning, the teacher teams can easily deliver intense small group instruction to those students needing extra help in mastering basics. A goal for any K–8 school must be that all students will succeed.

The maximum end of the curriculum in the sixth and seventh grade can be an exciting array of special short courses (minicourses) that address academic specialization, interest expansion, hobbies, or occupational projection. For years, middle schools have offered short-courses like "French for tourists," "short-wave (ham) radio," "the geometry of quilting," or "understanding household plumbing." Parents and community members can become heavily involved in this maximum end of the curriculum. Such courses can be delivered on the school grounds or in the halls even during lunch (the corridor curriculum). Such courses often provide a strong rationale for the content previously learned in Grades 2–5.

The eighth grade represents a capstone experience for all students, regardless of their state-tested academic progress. The teams of the sixth and seventh grade can be formed into even smaller learning communities entering the eighth grade, and those communities will consist of action learning teams made up of teachers, students, parents, and volunteers. In the eighth grade, students will apply the knowledge and skills they have been mastering since kindergarten, by engaging in service projects and community problem solving.

In the past, American education has demonstrated time and again the power of learning in the community (Wiles & Bondi, 2007). Under such conditions, parents can become serious learning partners and service clubs in the community (e.g., Kiwanis or Rotary) can demonstrate their primary roles with student assistance. Mentorships for leadership roles and occupational experience are also a major option during this time. If state testing is conducted at the eighth grade, such service learning can be used to tune up understanding of skills and knowledge.

Students in the eighth grade of the new K–8 school can and will experience democracy in action as they participate in community events and help fix things where they live. Regardless of their achievement level or skill mastery level, they will have a meaningful role as a young adult and as a future citizen.

Finally, in the eighth grade, student use of the Internet should become quite sophisticated. Learning and schooling should begin to transition to an "anytime, anyplace" status. Schooling is preparation for life and, for many students, that life is just around the corner. The goal of any K–8 curriculum is a self-sustaining and confident learner (see Figure 5.2).

Figure 5.2 Student experiences in the K–8 school

PreK	Planned readiness training by parents and preschool agencies
K–1	Social development Conceptual foundations Skill readiness activities Identification of learning challenges Planned physical development
2–5	Mastery of foundational knowledge Mastery of skills for continued learning Meet or exceed grade-level standards Social development activities
6–7	Placement on family teams Minimum–maximum curriculum options Opportunities for flexible grouping Academic specialization options
8	Small learning communities and action teams Service learning Simulation of democratic living Advanced Internet study

TEACHERS

Teachers in the new K–8 school will operate in one or more of the four tiers of development. At the K–1 level, teachers may be paired, or they may operate in a self-contained classroom. The teacher, as the "second parent," will be responsible for helping each child become acclimatized to school and institutional settings, develop social skills, receive an introduction to basic knowledge concepts, and begin the process of becoming skill literate. They will also serve as the "school eyes" to identify learning problems early.

The K–1 teachers will work very closely with parents to guarantee a positive experience for each child. The K–1 teacher can serve as the school's liaison to preK agencies and to the parents of future students. Teachers at this level may choose to "loop up" with students, thereby providing two years of close supervision at the start of the school years.

Teachers in the Grades 2–5 tier will have full responsibility for student literacy. Students in Grades 2–5 will follow the core subject and skill development profiles mandated by state standards. In addition, teachers in

Grades 2–5 will teach learning skills and technology skills so that the students will be capable of greater independent learning when they enter the sixth grade. The work of teachers in Grades 2–5 is all-important to the overall credibility of the K–8 design.

Teachers in the second tier will work largely in self-contained classrooms and teach in a traditional way, but the students may rotate out to other teachers for subject specialties. Multiage or nongraded classes are an option in Grades 2–5, as students can be assigned by skill attainment and learning needs, rather than age. Some teachers may choose to be paired (social studies with language arts, math with science) in order to specialize in their teaching. There should be considerable contact with parents, in person or via e-mail, to insure that each student is achieving at grade-level competence or, at least, to the best of their developmental ability.

Teachers in the Grade 6–7 tier will probably prefer to teach as a team so that students needing personal attention (minimum–maximum curriculum) can be serviced adequately.

The role of the teacher at this level is more of a learning coach, regardless of the level of achievement by the student. At the higher performance levels, these teachers will demonstrate how disciplines are applied and provide short-courses to practice learning skills. Students leaving this level should be capable of joining a community of learners and inquiring into social problems beyond the school.

Teachers in the 6–7 tier will work closely with parents and community members in planning enrichment activities. It is envisioned that teams of teachers in 6–7 will use interdisciplinary instruction and community-based lessons to bring together the many subjects and skills for students.

Finally, teachers in the eighth grade will be housed in *learning communities*, or learning teams, that will be made up of several smaller *action learning teams*. These learning communities and action teams will work with practical applications of the curriculum in school and out in the community. Students in such teams will use technology to gather independent data and will follow their teachers and community leaders into the field to participate in service projects and other community problem-solving efforts. Many field experiences may include occupational dimensions such as short internships and apprenticeships.

Eighth grade teachers will need to have greater in-depth content expertise so that connections can be made, as needed, to the academic subjects of high school and to more complex social issues (space program, health reform, etc.) during the year (see Figure 5.3). Advanced academic experiences can be designed for those students who might benefit from more in-depth work.

Figure 5.3   Teacher experiences in the new K–8 School

1. Will teach to standards specific goals
2. Will maintain student achievement profiles
3. Will experience better parental contact and cooperation
4. Will have the ability to meet individual student needs
5. Will have multiple roles

ADMINISTRATORS

Administration in the new K–8 school will reflect the blending of elementary and middle school programs. Seven areas of concern will dominate administrative activity as the program operates. Proper management of these areas will produce exciting model K–8 programs.

1. Parents

2. Community

3. Technology

4. Subject content

5. Schedules

6. Resources

7. Assessment

As stated throughout this book, parents will be important to the success of the K–8 school. Parents can be built-in as learning partners for the entire nine years, but the roles of parents at the various levels will have to be carefully delineated. In K–1, parents can be teacher assistants as they have always been. In 2–5, parents can become more like home-based teachers under the direction of classroom teachers. The Internet (e-mail) will allow close communication and instruction for parents that was never before possible (see Resource D). In Grades 6–7, parents will become school and community teaching partners, coming into classrooms and helping teachers organize instruction beyond the school. Finally in eighth grade, parents will often be in instructional roles in the field, with the classroom teacher being more of an academic coach and learning team leader.

The orientation, encouragement, and training of parents to serve in these roles will be the direct responsibility of the K–8 administrator. Parents who normally begin to withdraw after the fifth grade must be encouraged to share their knowledge and expertise from the real world beyond the school. Keeping the curriculum relevant and success-oriented for all students is the key to parental participation.

Being involved in the community is not a new role for elementary and middle school administrators, but the degree of activity that might take place in the community will require increased communication. The public must understand the sequential, developmental unfolding of the curriculum and why the curriculum should find final application out in the community. Media will play an important role in developing understanding in the community.

Technology, as outlined in this book, will also play a vital role for study and communication in the new K–8 school. As noted, most parents of school children now have an Internet connection, and the simple use of e-mail will allow the school to work directly with parents from their home. As of 2005, 94% of all public school classrooms had Internet access (National Center for Educational Statistics, United States Department of Education, 2008). Conferences, projections of instructional activities, student assessment, and the many other facets of school life can and should be accessible online through Web pages or other postings.

Technology will be the key to involving parents as instructional partners during those critical years when core information and basic literacy are transmitted (Grades 2–5). Even if parents don't feel competent in this role, their concern and knowledge will strengthen the program. Training programs for parents through the PTA or other similar groups will enhance this communication. Technology is also the key to students becoming independent learners by the sixth to seventh grade, and for learning communities to function smoothly in the eighth grade.

The suggested content for the K–8 differs from the past, when literacy was taught in the elementary grades and repeated again in middle school. This practice produced low achievement and highly unsatisfactory social patterns. In the new K–8 school, the first two years will be concerned with social adjustment and mastering basic learning tools. Grades 2–5 will focus solely on the input of critical information (for citizenship) and general literacy (for citizenship). Grades 6–7 will insure additional time for the mastery of such knowledge and skills, and for the enrichment of the curriculum for all students. In Grade 8, the content and skills mastered during the first 8 years (K–7) will be applied in the real world.

Administrators can insure that all students become minimally competent during their K–8 experience by using curriculum maps. State standards can serve as adequate benchmarks for the mastery of core information and learning skills. State testing at Grades 3, or 5, or 8 can also reveal how successful individual teachers are in reaching these minimal standards. Curriculum alignment and active management of the curriculum is a major responsibility of K–8 leaders.

More important for a successful program, however, is that the content and skills be taught in sequence as outlined in the four developmental stages. The ultimate goal of the K–8 school is a future citizen who possesses skills and knowledge, who can work with others, and who uses what he or she has learned to live in society as a contributing citizen. The focus of the curriculum in K–8 is general and applied knowledge. The common denominator among all the students is not subject mastery, but the learning skills and thinking skills they have learned to use. By taking such an approach to curriculum management, the traditional schism found in both the junior high school and the middle school, the academics versus personal growth arguments, can be avoided.

Scheduling the new K–8 school will require constant attention by administrators because the internal schedules will not look the same at all four levels. Paired teachers, grade-level teams, interdisciplinary teams of teachers, and small learning communities will use time differently within the schedule, and teachers will manage student learning in different ways. Both the block schedule of the middle school programs and the self-contained classroom schedule of traditional elementary teachers will work well in the new K–8 school. The important point is that the control of time, at all four levels, will need to be decentralized and given to the teachers. Elementary and middle school teachers are capable of such classroom leadership.

K–8 schools will need some new kinds of resources to be fully implemented, and these resources should be a part of any conversion planning (see Chapter 6). As we have seen, technology will be very important in this new 21st century school. K–1 students will need learning labs to master basic computer skills. Students in Grades 2–5 will need access to in-classroom computers for skill development and content retrieval. The sixth and seventh grade classrooms will require as many computers as possible so that students can have individualized experiences according to their readiness. In the eighth grade, students will need laptops and hand-held computing devices for field study and communication.

Administrators in the new K–8 school will have to make the case for these expensive learning tools and their support components. District administrators will need to understand the intention of the K–8 curriculum and the way that technology can free schools from the age-old problem of student diversity. It is no longer necessary for all students to travel together, lock-step, through the grade-level curriculum. Resources from other areas can be diverted to this most important resource.

Studies of previous K–8 conversions (Capistrano, 2008) show that K–8 schools can save districts money by limiting the number of administrators, support staff, and custodians. Leaders of K–8 schools should use such studies to advocate for additional resources in areas of need such as technology, libraries, and academic laboratories. K–8 schools should not cost additional funds from district budgets.

Resources will also be needed for any field-based learning beginning with K–1 field trips and continuing through eighth grade service-learning experiences. Such resources should be calculated into the operational budget of any K–8 program. To ignore such a budget item is to once again simply warehouse students in a different grade-level combination.

Finally, K–8 administrators are going to have to help teachers develop meaningful assessment instruments for measuring learning. K–8 schools will use state achievement testing as one measure of reaching mandated standards in subjects and learning skills. To supplement this kind of gross measurement, K–8 schools must develop detailed assessments of skill achievement, work portfolios, and a profile of experience by the student in his or her study.

Communication with parents about student progress should be continuous, rather than periodic, with parents using an assigned personal identification number to access their child's records. Any examples of work, or assignments, could be shared with parents using e-mail attachments. Prescriptions for remediation or achievement could be transmitted the same way. A paperless record trail would show schools drawing parallel to other 21st century institutions.

Administrators in K–8 schools can be confident that the schools they are developing will be better for students in attendance. Research clearly shows they are more effective, for whatever reason, and such schools meet parental expectation for full participation in the lives of their children while in school.

QUESTIONS FOR STUDY GROUPS

1. How can parents be made to feel a part of the new K–8 school in the upper grades?

2. What will the widespread usage of the Internet in the United States allow schools to do that they couldn't do previously?

3. What are some sample service-learning projects in your community that eighth graders might be involved in?

4. How would teachers act differently at each of the four designated tiers in the K–8 school?

5. What kind of a schedule could be used to organize learning throughout the K–8 school?

SUMMARY

Combining the best of the elementary school with the best of the middle school to form the new K–8 school will require considerable work. To create a true 21st century school, nearly every facet of the school will require change. The benefits of such efforts, the return on investment, will be considerable and well worth doing. The new K–8 school will service all students and produce citizens who are literate and who participate in our democracy.

The return for parents will be a school that serves every child well. It will also be a school that welcomes parental participation at every level. Parents will serve as teacher helpers, learning partners, community resources, and service-learning guides in the community.

Students will experience a developmentally appropriate curriculum that stretches to accommodate student diversity (minimum–maximum). In addition to literacy, all students will explore knowledge and develop thinking skills that will make them fully participating citizens.

Teachers will be teamed in different ways to serve students effectively. The role of teachers will be varied depending on the level of development they are assigned to teach.

Administrators will become curriculum designers and managers of the new learning program. They will organize parents and community, provide new technologies for learning, and monitor student progress through new assessment tools.

REFERENCES

Brumfield, R. (2005, May 24). *Ed visionaries: Schools must change.* Retrieved February 11, 2009, from the eSchool News Web site, http://www.eschoolnews.com/news/top-news/index.cfm?i=36370&CFID=5991669&CFTOKEN=36924229

Capistrano Unified School District. (2009). *San Juan Capistrano, California, K–8 conversions.* Retrieved February 22, 2009, from www.capousd.org

eSIS Parent Assistant. (n.d.). Retrieved February 11, 2009, from the St. Johns County Schools, Florida, Web site https://parents.stjohns.k12.fl.us and from the Student Information System, http://esis.nn.k12.va.us/about.htm

Core Knowledge Foundation. (2005). *Content guidelines for grades K–8.* Charlottesville, VA: Author.

Greenwood, G. (1993, January). Research and practice in parent involvement: Implications for teacher involvement. *Elementary School Journal, 91*(3), 279–286.

International Telecommunications Union. (2008). *Internet world status: Usage and population statistics.* Retrieved February 11, 2009, from www.internetworld-stats.com

Steyer, J. (2002). *The other parent.* New York: Atria Books.

Wiles, J., & Bondi, J. (2007). Parkway schools, Philadelphia public schools. In *Curriculum development: A guide to practice* (pp. 267–295). Englewood Cliffs, NJ: Prentice Hall.

Implementing the New K–8 Program

The full implementation of an appropriate K–8 program may take years, but it can be initiated today. In constructing new K–8 programs, educational leaders at the elementary and middle school level have one more opportunity to "get it right." The development of the new American K–8 school can serve as a source of renewal for entire school districts and communities.

We know a great deal about how curriculum development should proceed (Wiles, 2008), and in this chapter the basic tasks for implementing the suggested program will be outlined for administrators and teachers. The process is a deductive one, beginning with an end in mind and working backwards in ever greater detail. A first step, however, is the "big picture," where the before-and-after is displayed for consideration (see Figure 6.1).

The reader can think of this big picture as a kind of staging, in which the steps that are required in a number of defined areas are set out leading from the status quo to the desired condition. Between these two poles are the tasks that will activate the changes. At this point in planning for change, the leader is not concerned with the order of change or the timing of change, but just *what* will change. We also should not be concerned with any "yes, buts," or other negative arguments for why we can't change at this point. Keep in mind the old saying, "If you always do what you've always done, you'll always get what you've always got."

THE UNFOLDING PROCESS

Change in schools doesn't happen easily because school leaders rarely control all of the important variables that affect change such as the budget,

Figure 6.1   Early staging—before and after

	Before	Tasks	After
Facility	• Standard appearance • "Cells and bells" • Business look	• Soften with welcome entry • Casual eating areas • Connect to community • Lab-work spaces • New technologies	• Open to community • Relaxed atmosphere • Common learning areas • Teacher planning spaces • Safe and clean
Curriculum	• Standard subjects • Follow standards and testing • Grade "lock-step"	• Streamline content down to big ideas and key learning skills • Focus on Grades 5–7 • Four tiers model • Minimum–maximum options	• Developmentally appropriate • Focus on learning skills, general education, success for all
Teachers	• Deployed by grade and subject • Varied training • Focus on standards and testing	• Staff development • Assignment by role • Certification issues • Subscheduling	• Variety of teams • Multiple roles • Focused on skills • Closer to parents
Resources	• Traditional budget • Single library • School-based learning routines	• Money for field operations and technology • Greater variety in classroom materials • Community support	• Budget matches the instructional program • Community support for field-based learning • Reallocate budget for new technologies
Schedules	• 6 periods or modified block	• Block schedule with modifications for 4 tiers	• New time configurations, flexible length for instruction
Parents-Community	• Low involvement or noncurricular tasks	• New roles such as mentors, action-team members, home teacher	• Fully involved in instructional support K–8 • True partner

curriculum requirements, personnel, and facilities. Change efforts also must fully involve teachers who will ultimately implement any new program. The program projected in this book for the new K–8 school is heavily dependent on parents and community members for support and contribution. Finally, this proposed curriculum is a "break the mold" design that seeks to overcome the century-old weakness of intermediate education; trying to maintain a balance between general education and academic specialization.

Each subarea, outlined in Figure 6.1, will have some implementation tasks of varied length and complexity. Assessment of all progress will require a plan (see Chapter 7). Some of these tasks will be dependent upon the completion of prior tasks, and so any plan for implementing change is like a puzzle. In this section, we will examine the pieces of that puzzle prior to putting it all together.

PREREQUISITE CONDITIONS

Developing K–8 programs may be a districtwide initiative, but it will always be a school-level task. Because no two K–8 schools will have the same conditions or resources, each school program will be unique when implemented. School-based leaders should make every attempt to be involved in the general planning for K–8 schools at the district level. The input of the K–8 school leader should focus on three things.

1. Real curriculum change is needed in Grades K–8, not just grade realignments

2. Education is about general education and relevant education for all students

3. Individual schools will need freedom to develop a new kind of K–8 program

If senior administrators can see the K–8 initiative as an opportunity for true reform, and understand the historic mission of elementary and middle schools, change will come more easily. To the degree that senior administrators and school board members focus on recommended changes for the 21st century, the new curriculum can be more readily accepted and supported.

In addition to making input to the planning process in the early stages, school-based leaders should possess the basic knowledge and data to rationalize their recommended changes. An early needs assessment should tell the leader about existing conditions (i.e., dropouts, grade distributions, behavior problems, and parent opinions). Additional information, such as community support, preschool experiences of children in the community, the kind of learning challenges that students face, and community readiness for change (gathered from questionnaires), should be readily in hand. Any change in education must be rationalized as necessary to be successful.

Likewise, a clear and data-driven profile of the instructional pattern presently in place should be handy. What kinds of learning materials are found in your classrooms? How many computers (stand-alones, laptops, handheld) are available for student use? What sort of training have teaching staff experienced in the past 3 years?

School-based leaders would be wise to have canvassed the community to assess support for a new kind of program. Given the current pressure from parents across the nation to leave middle schools and construct community K–8 schools, it should be easy to document what the constituents of school board members and senior leaders want for children in their community. Be prepared to hand out the list of 20 reasons why K–8 schools make sense, presented earlier in Chapter 1.

Clear Mission Statement

Prior to any curriculum change, the K–8 leader should be able to state clearly the objective of that desired change. A sample statement from one Connecticut K–8 school read

The goal of the K–8 school is to produce a future citizen who possesses skills and knowledge, who can work with others, and who uses what he or she has learned to live in society as a contributing member.

The K–8 leader should be ready to share with others the set of beliefs that undergird any planned change effort. From the Bedrock Beliefs (Figure 1.6), the leader can share that K–8 educators believe the following:

1. Learning should be developmentally appropriate

2. All students should experience success in school

3. The value of subject matter is found in its utility

4. Families and the community should be partners in school learning

5. Students should be prepared for 21st century life

Be prepared to back up these beliefs with resources and statements from commissions like the 21st Century Skills Group, the Carnegie Corporation, and the U.S. Department of Labor.

Finally, the school-based leader should be able to clearly define any terms that might be used to describe the intended school program. Parents and community leaders might not fully comprehend terms like general education, learning coaches, mentoring, curriculum maps, action learning, and looping. Resource D provides a glossary of such terms.

Concise Description of the Curriculum

The curriculum of K–8 schools is based on the developmental patterns of learners from ages 5–13. These stages are early childhood (Grades K–1), later childhood (Grades 2–5), preadolescence (Grades 6–7), and sometimes adolescence (Grade 8). The K–8 curriculum will be organized in four tiers or stages, following the developmental level of the students, and each learning tier will be unique in its organization and purpose. The general flow of the curriculum through the four tiers is from orientation to mastery, and from mastery to expansion and application. The program will want to help students become people possessing knowledge and skills who can use those tools in life after school.

Parts of the curriculum will include content from state learning standards, various academic, social, life, technical, and workforce skills, and various methodologies that will encourage and teach cooperative learning and ethical behaviors. The state standards can organize the curriculum boundaries in each tier because most are broken into similar developmental levels.

The learning skills and thinking skills that run through all four tiers of the curriculum are the common denominators for all students. The academic achievement of students will have a range of about a year for each year in school, and students will have varied grade-level mastery of content. Although the students will be studying content in varying degrees of sophistication, all students will be taught common learning skills used to assess that knowledge.

Figure 6.2 illustrates the kind of academic learning skills, thinking skills, and technical skills that students will master and use during the K–8 period. Figure 6.3 suggests social, life, and work-related skills that students will encounter in the new K–8 curriculum.

Ten common instructional practices will be used to encourage access to the curriculum and to promote collaboration in learning. General access to learning will be supported by a differentiated curriculum, the use of flexible time schedules, and interdisciplinary content lessons. Personal student access to learning will be supported by recognition of multiple intelligences, learning styles, and looping of teachers who know and understand the student.

Figure 6.2   Learning skills, thinking skills, and technical skills

Learning Skills	Thinking Skills	Technical Skills
Reading	Asking questions	Using visual technologies
Writing	Making comparisons	Creating media
Computation	Ranking	Networking
Listening	Reforming knowledge	Creating publishing products
Recalling information	Problem solving	Collaborative work
Accessing information	Making judgments	Workplace applications
Using a home study routine	Defining issues	Research and writing
Paraphrasing	Gaining perspective	
Explaining information		
Analyzing information		
Assessing word meanings		
Doing computer searches		
Organizing		

Figure 6.3   Social skills, life skills, and workplace skills

Social Skills	Life Skills	Workplace Skills
Playing with others	Deferring judgment	Constructing solutions
Accepting differences	Consensus building	Working with others
Sex role identification	Guessing solutions	Managing time
Requesting help	Decision making	Resolving conflicts
Respecting others	Sharing knowledge	Behaving safely
Challenging ideas	Having a positive outlook	
Being empathetic	Holding a world view	
Value clarification	Having an occupational projection	
Acting ethically	Dressing appropriately	
Being future oriented	Interviewing	
Having high self-esteem		
Being honest		

Collaboration in learning, preparation for 21st century work, will be supported by cooperative learning methodologies, group problem-based learning (action learning), the use of adult and student mentors, and community-based service learning experiences.

Five areas of special interest in developing the new K–8 curriculum include the minimum–maximum feature in Grades 6–7, streamlining state content standards, the common skill continuums running from Kindergarten through the eighth grade, the "big idea" experiences planned for K–1, and the collaboration activities found in all grades.

By far the most dramatic feature of the new K–8 program would be the minimum–maximum curriculum found in Grades 6 and 7. This instrument would address the ever-widening range of achievement in the upper grades and allow teachers to serve students where we find them. Our pledge to students at the minimum end of achievement is that they will receive special instruction in small groups in order to complete basic skill mastery. In effect, these students can take from second grade through seventh grade to master four years of the regular curriculum.

For students who have already completed the literacy portion of the curriculum, these years can be spent receiving in-depth content study, exploring personal areas of academic interest, expanding talents, or otherwise connecting school learning to the real world. These options, much like the electives "wheel" experiences in the middle school, would be of short duration and probably not graded. Students would maintain a portfolio of these experiences.

Another area of the curriculum to be constructed would include insuring that the state content standards are followed in each grade. Most states have done a fine job of identifying that knowledge to be covered grade-by-grade, and most of these continuums are grouped by developmental level. Each school may wish to streamline these lists (see Chapter 2) and add or delete items as fits the school population. It is envisioned that a curriculum mapping process (Hale, 2007) could be used to accomplish this task.

A third area of development in the curriculum is to take the many academic, social, and work-related skills list in Figures 6.2 and 6.3 and form them into a grade-targeted continuum (i.e., grade-level expectation). This work is important because teachers in the upper grades can build on academic skills mastered in Grade K–5. These skills would be mastered at both an understanding and application level by all students, regardless of their general achievement levels in the state standards.

A fourth curriculum task would be to view the entire K–8 curriculum for outcomes and work backward (Wiggins & McTighe, 2001)) to the K–1 level. In the first learning tier, students will be given conceptual experiences that lead to further content study or even action learning experiences in the upper grades. It is vitally important to the overall outcome for this "spiral" feature to be coordinated. The reader may want to revisit Figure 3.1, "Big Ideas," to think about what K–1 experiences would introduce understanding of ideas such as *living things, citizenship,* or *relationships.*

Finally, the K–8 curriculum should teach collaboration extensively as preparation for 21st century living. The various cooperative learning techniques should be infused throughout the K–5 curriculum, and group work, group problem-solving, and group work using technology should be heavily emphasized in the upper grades (see Figure 6.4).

Figure 6.4   Special areas of the new K–8 curriculum

Conceptual experiences in K–1

Streamlined state content standards

K–8 thinking skills continuum

Minimum–maximum in Grades 6 and 7

Collaboration in all grades

New Parental Roles

The new K–8 curriculum will be characterized by the degree of parent involvement. School leaders in new K–8 programs must remember that it has been parent pressure on schools that has forced this new pattern. Parents want safe, personal, productive, and accessible schools for their children at this level of education. The K–8 school should acknowledge the influence that parents can have on achievement of students and use this valued resource to the fullest (see Figure 6.5).

This book has noted that parents have always been a strong influence in the K–1 tier as room mothers and fathers, field trip chaperones, and

Figure 6.5   Involving parents in the school

As aides, chaperones, and helpers

As partners at home via e-mail

As academic progress monitors

As mentors and speakers

As action learning team members

As developers of experiences

As advocates in the community

as providers of extra resources for learning. It is hoped that this timeless relationship will continue between the parents of young children and the teachers of young children.

A much larger role is being projected for parents in the second, third, and fourth tiers of the K–8 curriculum. Capitalizing on the fact that nearly three-quarters of all Americans have Internet access in their homes—perhaps more for the parents of school children—schools can now reach out to parents as never before. Parents can be at-home learning partners and progress monitors for their children, and there is even a possibility that some parents could be active in finding online resources for the K–8 school.

In the upper grades, parents can have an even greater role in curriculum and instruction. Parents can serve as learning mentors to children in the minimum–maximum tier. They can be classroom resources in the sixth and seventh grade exploratory programs. They can serve as action learning team members in the eighth grade and help connect the school to service club projects. Parents can also help develop out-of-building learning experience in the community (i.e., develop curriculum) and serve as speakers to advocate for the K–8 school program in the community.

It is clear that schools, for whatever reasons, have never used the power of parents in the manner proposed in this book. It is worth mentioning that one of the major reasons given by parents for becoming home-schoolers is the desire to be an active partner in their child's schooling experience!

Different Roles for Teachers

The teachers of the new K–8 school will come from different training backgrounds (elementary or intermediate) and they will have slightly different conceptions of what a teacher does.

Elementary teachers will be broadly prepared in most subject areas and have more knowledge about the development of children. Those teachers coming from middle schools will have less knowledge of all but one or two content areas and less preparation in methods of teaching.

Middle school teachers will know a great deal about preadolescents, and they will know one or more subjects well. These varied backgrounds of K–8 teachers are an asset for the four-tier K–8 curriculum, because teacher roles will change as the student progresses through school.

To the degree that their certification will allow, teachers in Grades K–5 should be allowed to select their tier in terms of their self-perceived skills. K–1 teachers will have a dual role of introducing learning and teaching basic skills. Teachers in Grades 2–5 will teach more like traditional school teachers, but will need to work closely with parents and possess advanced technology skills.

Former middle school teachers will choose between a role of minimum–maximum teacher, teaching either remediation or exploratory short-courses, or the role of action team leader in a learning community. In the latter role, the teacher will also need to be an academician capable of bridging student learning to high school preparation. It is anticipated that the K–8 placement of teachers, for certification purposes, will be most difficult in the sixth grade. The reader will want to review grade-level eligibility for the elementary certificate, middle school endorsement, and secondary certificate in his or her state.

Reconceptualizing the school program at the K–8 level will prove very hard for some teachers because their experience has been in more traditional programs. Teacher training in universities presupposes that content is the organizer for the curriculum. The idea of a developmental curriculum with four tiers may seem strange. The notion of parents as teaching and learning partners will be foreign to most teachers. Being a teacher in the classroom, online, and in the community will be a challenging idea. The teachers *must* be on board if this program is to succeed, and that means that a lot of insightful staff development will be required.

The best staff development is when teachers train other teachers. Staff development is most effective and received most favorably when teachers participate in the development of the experience and are involved in the choice of learning experiences. For K–8 leaders, it should be obvious that staff development or in-service should be directed toward program development and that teachers should be able to participate where they want in learning how to implement the program,

Some teachers, for example, may be fascinated by the minimum–maximum feature. Other teachers may want to work on the parent participation dimension, or the K–8 skill continuum, or the community learning. All teachers in the school should be familiar with the ten key methods for involving students. Certainly, teachers should receive training within the mission of their tier. Teachers with advanced technology capabilities can be "near-peer" mentors to their colleagues. As noted earlier, the K–8 program represents an opportunity for all staff members to grow, and their conceptual contributions about the way the program can be should be welcomed (see Figure 6.6).

By the same token, parents can be offered training that will allow them to become a valuable resource to the K–8 school. Parents will need to understand human development, the flow of the curriculum, ways to communicate with the school about their child's progress, how evaluation will be handled, and ways to participate as a helper in off-campus learning or as an at-school mentor. The best training will feature parents training other parents.

Figure 6.6   Preparing teachers for the K–8 school

Selection of teaching tier
Understanding the new developmental design
Appropriate staff development opportunities
Working in areas of choice for implementation

Acquiring Resources

The acquisition of resources for the K–8 school will prove a difficult task in today's economy. Throughout the United States, schools are cutting programs and releasing teachers in order to balance budgets. Certainly, the leader of a new K–8 school must be an advocate for the program and be informed when presenting ideas to superiors.

The general scenario for gaining commitment to this new program must be the stark realities of education in public and private intermediate schools, particularly in urban and rural areas. As noted earlier, some schools are failing students very badly in these environments.

Educators continue to provide a curriculum for a population that never existed, while ignoring the basic citizenship requirements of today's world. The new K–8 curriculum is a direct response to the needs of our society, now and in the future. Pressing problems must be addressed.

The three major resource needs for operating a program such as the one proposed in this book are money for technology, money for learning materials, and money for out-of-school learning experiences. Presently, in the United States, a full 80% of public school operating funds go to teacher salaries and facilities. In order to convert our existing school programs to a modern 21st century model, we may have to unlock some of these funds.

Few of the existing K–8 schools are operating in new buildings, and a lot of arguments for converting to K–8 buildings claim a savings in facilities and personnel. Although this may or may not be true, K–8 leaders should point this out to superiors while arguing for more resources. One might also argue that the intermediate grades, in most states, are underfunded, and that this is where most of the curriculum work will be done in the K–8 school. Finally, it is a fact that Grades 5–8 have the lowest achievement on norm-referenced standardized tests in the United States. It can be argued that the upper grades of the new K–8 school are the greatest cause of low district achievement, and investment is warranted.

Due to high unionism in urban areas, the topic of teacher salaries is a sacred cow at budget time. But if leaders in new K–8 schools look at this issue carefully, they will find that not filling a position ($50,000, with in-kind costs), even for a year, can help their school acquire new technologies. If filling one teaching position is suspended for only one year in a building with 400 students and 20 teachers, thereby raising the pupil–teacher ratio by one student, two classrooms worth of computers can be purchased. If that vacancy can be left open for three years, your school is technologically ready for the 21st century (Wiles & Bondi, 2007).

In many urban and rural school districts, Technology Literacy Challenge Grants and federal E-Rate programs have supplied many computers for classrooms. However, many of these learning tools are stand-alone models placed in computer laboratories. These computers will work well for the computer training in the lower grades of the new K–8 schools, but laptops and wireless mobile devices are more appropriate for the 21st century. In fact, such hardware is essential for a modern school. Beyond government programs and corporate gifts, K–8 leaders will have to begin trading-off 20th century resources for 21st century resources.

In addition to money for mobile learning instruments critical to field-based learning, leaders will also need to find additional resources for in-class instructional materials.

In particular, because of the range of student achievement, this school will need large amounts of learning resources at varying readability levels. Many new K–8 schools may find these materials if they are careful in the closing and combining of elementary and middle schools. It is the author's experience, however, that such "collecting" requires a plan to be successful.

Again, thinking about the 21st century school, the obvious source of funds for such additional materials may come from library resources. Libraries will always be important to educated people, but increasingly our source of knowledge is found online rather than in deposited or stored knowledge. How many readers, we might ask, go to the library for factual answers, and how many use Google? Librarians are quickly making this transition to the new age.

On a final note, the new learning materials selected should be developmentally appropriate for the tier, should have realistic readability levels, should be culturally sensitive, and should be relevant to the lives of learners. Student use of these materials, not storing them, is the ultimate goal of securing them.

The last resource need is funding to operate field or community learning. These would include K–1 field trips, 6–7 exploratory activities, and Grade 8 community service learning. Many of these experiences can be planned in proximity to the school itself, thereby reducing any transportation needs. Still, armed with mobile technology and school and community mentors, these students will have resource needs. Schools may explore portable lunches on field days. City transportation may be available for students, as in the Philadelphia Parkway programs (Bremer, 1971).

Consumable learning materials may be contributed by service clubs or other community resources.

Figure 6.7 summarizes the key learning materials for the new K–8 school. Failure to budget for these real learning resources may cause the quality of such experiences to detract from the program. Failure caused by being "a penny wise and a pound foolish" is all too common in American education.

Figure 6.7   Resource needs

Mobile technologies
Varied classroom learning materials
Field-based learning resources

Assessment

Assessment has always been the Achilles Heel of new programs. Not only do new programs need to rationalize changing from old programs, but they also must prove that such change was valuable. Middle school programs (6–8) in the United States, despite some glowing internal reviews by districts, do not have a strong evaluation record. To promote a lasting change, the new American K–8 school must prove its claims to be a superior form of education (see Chapter 7 for assessment outlines).

Assessment will come in the form of 3 Ps: *process, product,* and *performance.*

The process measures of any assessment will be concerned with what happened, seeing the existing program transforming into a new program. This measuring should be a validation of any goal setting and the implementation of any plan for changing (Chapter 7).

The product measure of assessment would look at the result of changing. Has the K–8 school met its goals and does it, in fact, resemble the projected program? If the program is implemented as planned, the result will be a product, the new K–8 school.

Finally, because this program was planned and developed into a product, the result should equal a different performance in students. This performance, or result, should be shown to be causal: because this change was made, we get this result. Most of the existing K–8 research is not of this nature.

School leaders in new K–8 programs should document existing conditions and verify changes to new program standards. They should also, early on, project changes in the way students learn because of these new practices. Such documentation is the very best argument for more resources in the future. These conditions are currently rarely documented in schools. Failure to document will result in accomplishments being ignored and resources being withheld (see Figure 6.8).

Figure 6.8   Assessment requirements

Documentation of implementation steps
Documentation of design standards
Documentation of new achievements

PUTTING IT ALL TOGETHER

A basic curriculum development plan should contain an easily understood set of steps to change. Because of the natural change in schools, such as teacher turnover or new building principals, time is an important variable. The order of activities that promote change can be extremely important. What is needed for any school constructing a K–8 program is a simple visual that says, "Here is what we are going to do, in this order, and this is how long it will take." It is also very helpful to project, and then prove, a product.

The figures found in this chapter can form a basis for planning the new K–8 program. We can block out at least three stages of development from the tasks outlined in this chapter.

1. Preparation

2. Planning

3. Implementing (see Figure 6.9 for an implementation schedule)

After 24 months of planning, the school will begin parts of the pilot program during year 3. In the first round, this would be presented as 2 years of planning with limited implementation during year 3. Obviously, the entire implementation may take longer because curriculum change is like a distance-rate-time problem in math. The more resources that are applied (money), the faster the implementation proceeds.

As the new K–8 reaches the program development stage in year 3, individual schools will take on unique characteristics according to their resources, community, and energy levels. Individual sections of the curriculum will be highly refined, some more than others, and the program will be refined by K–8 leaders. A 21st century school will emerge serving all students as they learn to learn.

Figure 6.9 Implementation schedule for the K–8 program

Month 0	Month 12	Month 18	Month 24
Conduct needs assessment			
Develop clear mission statement	Rationalize with goals and objectives	Create detailed plan for each tier level	Finalize plan for activating program
Meet with superintendent, to project changes	Design field learning schedule	Develop community events	Activate trial field-based learning
Develop description of curriculum	Design five areas of curriculum	Develop five areas of curriculum	Develop teacher staff
Select and assign teachers to tiers	Plan technology for learning	Order and install technology	Technology training for parents and teachers
Form parent advisory group	Define roles for parents	parent curriculum group in place	
Establish baseline evaluation data	Establish assessment design	Complete student assessment instrument	Validate process steps

For educational leaders, the important thing to remember is that this level of education has been a problem child for nearly a century. The statistics are sad, and we have an opportunity to improve education at this level because of the K–8 movement. Students come to us uneven, and they will certainly leave us as a diverse group; they are just passing through. But all of the students at this level will be citizens, some sooner than others, and this agency called the school has the responsibility of preparing these students for adult living. The new K–8 model can master that challenge.

QUESTIONS FOR STUDY GROUPS

1. What are the advantages of thinking about school change in terms of stages?

2. How can skills best be organized as a common learning path for all students?

3. How can parents be encouraged to take a larger role in school curriculum matters?

4. What are the advantages and disadvantages of using teacher vacancies for purchasing technology?

SUMMARY

The process of creating a new school from combining elementary and middle schools will take planning and time. Such a curriculum development project can be a source of personal renewal for all faculty members at the school.

Staging out the change, and defining each area in terms of the major steps to be taken, can serve as the framework for a model of changing at the school. This design for Grades K–8 will require a comprehensive plan that may take more than three years to implement. Areas of concern would be the content, learning skills, teacher roles, student roles, schedules, and assessment devices.

Significant resources may be needed to implement the new K–8 plan, and these resources may come from existing sources rather than new sources. The design of a 21st century school for Grades K–8 will call for an open mind in planning.

REFERENCES

Bremer, J. (1971). *The school without walls: Philadelphia's Parkway Program.* New York: Holt, Rinehart & Winston. (Eric Document Reproduction Service No. ED059117)

Capistrano Unified School District. (n.d.). Retrieved February 11, 2009, from http://www.capousd.org/

Hale, J. (2007). *A guide to curriculum mapping.* Thousand Oaks, CA: Corwin.

Wiggins, G., & McTighe, K. (2001). *Understanding by design.* Englewood Cliffs, NJ: Prentice Hall.

Wiles, J. (2008). *Leading curriculum development.* Thousand Oaks, CA: Corwin.

Wiles, J., & Bondi, J. (2007). *Curriculum development: A guide to practice* (pp. 299–320). Englewood Cliffs, NJ: Prentice Hall.

Validating Progress

Throughout this book, the new K–8 school has been presented as a reaction to the status quo in elementary and middle schools in the United States. School leaders, parents, and even students appear to want a different and superior lower school. In the first six chapters, the various wants and needs of these groups have been delineated. This final chapter addresses how we monitor and validate our progress in developing the K–8 school.

Validation, as a process, is like keeping score. No judgments (evaluation) are made about the worth of a program, and K–8 education in the United States will have to wait for better research efforts to make such qualitative determinations. What we can do, at this point in time, is define K–8 education through the programs that we develop.

K–8 leaders should keep the history of junior high schools and middle schools squarely in their sights as they begin the validation process. Both of those forms of intermediate education grew rapidly, with much excitement, but soon lost their programmatic focus. Evaluation, or the lack of it in the case of those schools, proved the Achilles heel of their longevity.

Promoting the kind of change outlined in this book calls for a long-term commitment, resources, and significant energy. It will be important that we keep the ends in sight as we move along or we will surely become lost in myriad details of planning and execution.

In this chapter, the author offers a sketch of an assessment plan that can guide the development of quality K–8 schools.

Figure 7.1 only begins to sample the kind of work areas that principals and other K–8 leaders will have to consider in bringing desired changes to their new K–8 schools.

(Text continues on page 104)

Figure 7.1   K–8 item checklist for leaders

I Concept Development		
Item	*Action*	*Simple Evidence*
Assess needs	Assessing of available data	Achievement scores
		Discipline referrals
		Student attendance
		High school dropout rate
		Parent participation
		Suspensions
		Parent conferences
		Busing patterns and cost
		Student health indicators
		Violence reports (bullying)
		Teacher turnover
Existing resource inventory	Assess resources for use	Teacher certifications
		Computers by type
		Library inventory summary
		Instructional budget materials
		Facility floor plans
		Existing staff development
		Previous evaluation reports
Projective opinions	Assess attitudes about school	Student attitude inventories
		Parent attitudes about school
		Community participation
		Goals statements
		Public criticisms

II Mission Statements		
Item	*Action*	*Simple Evidence*
Case-building	Gather support data	Research summaries
		Innovative K–8 schools
		Goal statements from schools
		21st century visions for schools
		Expert opinions (newspapers)
		Educational Commission endorsements
		Key community endorsements
Bedrock beliefs	Stating premises	Belief statements
		Parent wish list
		Short mission statement
		Teacher union statement
		Simple K–8 goals
		Supporting state documents
Short case for K–8	Develop quick summary	Mission
		Rationale
		Support for concept
		Research support
		Five simple goals
III Curriculum Design		
Item	*Action*	*Simple Evidence*
Purpose statement	Formulating general education	Statement of case for general education
		Role of content clarified
		State standards structures
		Human development rationale

(Continued)

(Continued)

Item	Action	Simple Evidence
Development	Including features	Continuum of learning skills
		Internet delivery
		Articulation with preK and high school programs
		Maps-standards compliance
		4 learning levels (tiers) defined
		Minimum–maximum options, Grades 6–7
		10 practices to activate
		Safety emphasis
Libraries	Define library	Holdings
		Locations
		Uses of technology
Schedules	Create internal schedule	General schedule
		Minimum–maximum schedules
		Service learning and problems-based learning Other sub-schedules
Assessment	Analyze students	State testing
		Sample student portfolios
		Parental monitoring of student work

IV Instructional Features

Item	Action	Simple Evidence
Student deployment	Define the 4 tiers	Definition of program for K–1, 2–5, 6–7, 8 levels
		Minimum–maximum options
		Sequenced learning
		Individual portfolios (electronic or paper)

Item	Action	Simple Evidence
		Parents as study partners
		Special "growing up" curriculum for Grades 7–8
		Common life skills for all
		Varied grouping possibilities
		Learning challenges identification procedures
Nonstandard delivery	Creating options	Field trips
		Classroom
		Laboratories
		Minicourses
		Problem-based instruction
		Service learning
		Apprenticeships
		Internet assisted lessons

V Teachers

Item	Action	Simple Evidence
Selection and placement	Assigning teachers	Familiarity with all 4 tiers
		Certification appropriate
		Teaching styles considered
		New teacher job descriptions
		Recruitment procedures
Roles and tasks	Determining roles	Tier selection (one or more)
		Partnering with parents
		Self-contained, pairs, teams
		Training program

(Continued)

(Continued)

Item	Action	Simple Evidence
		Technology skills
		Academic dimensions
		Hobbies inventory
Training	Developing staff	Working with parents
		10 practices for implementing
		Records design and management
		Teaching basic skills
		Small group management
		Action learning

VI Parents

Item	Action	Simple Evidence
Communication	Orienting parents	Understand 4-tier design
		Involved in program definition
Participation	Designing parent roles	Different parent roles by stage
		Involving parents in instructional design
Training	In-service for parents	Human growth and development
		Profiling student growth
		Internet connections to school
		Monitoring child's learning
		Accessing student portfolios
		Onset of puberty Grades 5–8
		Special practices in K–8 school
		Parents as partners
		General education designs

VII Facilities and Transportation		
Item	*Action*	*Simple Evidence*
Modifications	Defining add-on specifications	Labs
		Special furniture needs
		Physical education needs
		Handicap modifications
		Library areas
	Features	Creating learning community areas
		Humanize foyer
		Activity areas and life skills
		Collaborative spaces
		Community access points
		Climate management
Transport needs	Finding special transports	Field trips
		Problem-based learning
		Service learning
		Community travel needs
VIII Technology		
Item	*Action*	*Simple Evidence*
Purchase plan	Define technology needs	Staggered schedule
		Priorities for learning
		Deployment
Parental access	Design access	Web pages
		Lock-outs
		Server usage
Teachers	Defining classroom use	Classroom use
		Field-based uses
		Communicate with home
		Storage of student portfolios
		Records design and management

Once a simple group of projects is selected, according to the school priorities, the projects are further placed into responsibility charts with task, person, and due dates identified. Activities should be spaced out over time with "rest periods" for reviewing progress. Leaders should organize such activities by working backwards from where they wish to be and what has to be accomplished to complete that specific part of the K–8 program.

Taking all of these things into consideration, each leader will have to design his or her own plan for developing the best K–8 school around. Above all else, curriculum development is successful when it is managed and validated on a regular basis.

Resource A

Summary of K–8 Research Findings

The research agenda for K–8 schools has been, from the beginning, exclusively comparative in nature. Because national studies have raised concerns about middle school academic performance (Carnegie, 1989; RAND Corporation, 2004; Trends in International Math and Science Study, 1999), K–8 research is generally framed within comparative middle school performance data.

Research that compares student performance in K–8 schools to student performance in traditional Grade 6–8 middle schools generally favors the K–8 school in all categories. Most researchers and school leaders agree, however, that many of the hundreds of studies that have been conducted in this manner cannot be substantiated for a number of reasons. Most studies have been conducted without traditional research controls or designs. Still, the vast majority of all studies that look at K–8 school performance, such as achievement, attendance, discipline, and participation, favor the K–8 school model.

From this large number of comparative studies, what emerges are three critical educational variables that seem to account for most differences in K–8 performance: school size, student transition patterns, and school environment. These variables suggest that the "magic" of K–8 education may result from conditions not accounted for in these studies. These conditions will serve as "reservations" to an otherwise overwhelming pattern of research support for the K–8 school.

RESERVATIONS

School Size

K–8 schools are considerably smaller than 6–8 middle schools throughout the nation. In one study of 304 K–8 schools, 81% had fewer than 600 students and the mean size was 426 students. Middle schools generally house about 1,000 students (McEwin, 2004).

A study of K–8 schools in Philadelphia found these schools to be smaller than 6–8 middle schools within the same district. The author concluded

> Philadelphia's K–8 schools serve fewer students per grade than middle grade schools, so they have fewer teachers per grade. They typically serve the students for nine years while middle schools serve them for three years. They tend to serve students who reside in smaller feeder neighborhoods than middle grade schools. These conditions allow K–8 schools more opportunities for teacher–teacher, teacher–student, and teacher–parent relations, and a more supportive interpersonal environment to evolve. (Offenberg, 2001, pp. 28–29)

A study by Duke University found the larger size of middle schools to be detrimental to any academic achievement, attendance, and social engagement. Middle schools were found to generally serve higher-minority and higher-poverty student populations than K–8 schools ("K–8 Comeback," 2008).

A researcher for a Johns Hopkins University study stated that "a straight-forward comparison of K–8 schools and middle schools achievement (in Philadelphia) is not wise, since students in K–8 schools are more likely than those in middle schools to be white and non-poor" (Balfanz, 2002).

Transitions

Numerous studies have credited fewer student grade transitions in a K–8 school for the increase in school performance. A major study in Baltimore City System found students who transitioned only after the eighth grade fared better in academics, especially in math (Yakimowski, 2001).

Alspaugh (1998) found a significant achievement loss for each transition made by students in school.

A study by Gronna (2006) documented achievement losses after transitions from elementary to middle grades.

School Environment

A study of Maine eighth graders attributed achievement decline to "considerations such as instructional specialization, tracking, with in-the-classroom ability grouping, expectations for student performance, and sensitivity to individual differences" (Howley, 2002).

A Wisconsin study found that the K–8 configuration more effectively supports student psychological growth into adolescence (Simmons & Blyth, 1987).

Typical middle school environments are associated with increases in teacher control, the number of teachers, pupils in a class, stricter grade scales, and a decrease in teacher support, teacher–student relationships, and teacher efficacy" (Barber, 2006).

Finally, as Colorado's Education Commissioner Moloney stated in 2008, "the longer students stay in one school, the more relationships they form with teachers and other adults. And, the more such relationships, the stronger the student's support system and likelihood of success."

BEST STUDIES

The reservations above might easily account for many of the differences in K–8 and 6–8 school performance comparisons. Evaluations of these studies suggest that we might be overlooking the effect of such items as transportation, nearness to home, effects of poverty, and time-on-task in many of these studies. Having presented these disclaimers, however, the overwhelming positive support for the K–8 model under all kinds of research studies is impressive. Below are found a number of widely cited studies that form the basis of research support for K–8 school models:

The strongest studies on K–8 performance, in terms of research design and control of variables are Offenberg's "The Efficacy of Philadelphia's K–8 Schools Compared to Middle Grade Schools" (2001), and Byrnes and Ruby's (2007) "Comparing Achievement Between K–8 and Middle Schools: A Large-Scale Empirical Study." Both of these studies used structured research data from the Philadelphia School District.

Offenberg collected data from 1996–1999 in about forty K–8 schools and forty middle schools in Philadelphia. The number of schools varied over time as conversions to K–8 took place. The study found that students in K–8 schools performed better than students in 6–8 middle schools on standardized measures such as the Stanford (SAT-9) achievement test and in all testing involving reading, math, and science to a statistically significant degree. K–8 students in Philadelphia also did better academically in the ninth grade. Reservations by the researchers are cited in the previous sections above.

The Byrnes and Ruby study (Johns Hopkins University) reviewed the same data from ninety-five Philadelphia schools involving 41,000 students and drew a more refined conclusion. They found that while K–8 students outperformed comparable middle schools, the advantage was only true in older K–8 schools with small enrollments and fewer minority and poverty students. After controlling the study for school transition and grade size, they found "no discernable differences in academic performance achievement between K–8 schools and middle schools."

In a research briefing for the School District of Philadelphia (Balfanz, 2002), it was observed that "When K–8 and middle schools that serve similar students from the same neighborhood are compared, no K–8 performance advantage on the PSSA is observed" (pp. 16). This review also cited school size as a significant factor in high academic achievement in Philadelphia.

Together, these two studies represent the best effort to objectively study the performance of the K–8 model in comparison to like populations in middle schools under highly controlled conditions. They certainly will contribute to the design of future studies.

As early as 1997, Paglin and Fager (Klump, 2006) were observing that K–8 studies were failing to control many factors and, therefore, results could be attributed to reasons other than grade configuration. Within this category are a number of in-house studies by school districts or states seeking to investigate or validate the K–8 model. The best known of these studies are listed below:

Alspaugh (1998)—In a study of sixteen rural school district documented that achievement dropped when students went from elementary to middle schools. He also found high school dropout rates were higher for students who had attended 6–8 middle schools.

Wihry (1992)—In a study of 163 schools in Maine, researchers found achievement on state tests were higher for K–8 students than when the students attended an eighth grade housed in a middle or high school.

Howley (2002)—In a Connecticut study it was found that students in sixth grade classes that were connected to an elementary school (K–6 or K–8) achieved higher test scores than students in sixth grades attached to junior or high schools.

Milwaukee—Studies in this school system determined that eighth graders in the K–8 pattern had a 4% increase in attendance and that suspensions for seventh graders were 9% higher in traditional middle schools when compared to the K–8 model (Milwaukee City Schools, Research Bulletin).

Portland—The school district in Portland found that students in the ninth grade with only one transition (at the eighth grade) had statistically significant higher GPAs than those who had attended separate middle schools (Portland Public Schools, Pulse Newletter).

Cleveland—reported that sixth grade students in K–8 schools scored higher in both reading and mathematics than those who had attended a middle school in the same district (Cleveland Public Schools, Research Bulletin).

Pittsburgh—This school district is reporting that African-American students in K–8 schools outperformed their peers in traditional middle schools in reading and math.

Baltimore—Found that eighth graders attending K–8 schools performed better in reading, language arts, and math than students attending middle schools as measured by CTB TerraNova tests.

Miami—Researchers (Abella, 2005) found that K–8 students have significant short-term gains in achievement, attendance, and suspension rates in the Dade County system.

CONCLUSION

The reader will note that there is "much smoke" in the various studies cited in this brief review. Although many of these studies may reflect an eagerness to justify a change in grade configuration in order to make a facilities change or serve a community demand for neighborhood school patterns, there seems to be convincing data everywhere that the K–8 school model influences student behavior. It is believed that more high quality studies will follow as this educational movement continues.

REFERENCES

Alspaugh, J. (1998). Achievement loss associated with the transition to middle school and high school. *Journal of Educational Research, 92*(1), 20–25.

Balfanz, R. (2002). *Will converting high-poverty middle schools to K–8 schools facilitate achievement gains?* Baltimore: Johns Hopkins University.

Barber, B. (2006). Assessing the transitions to middle school and high school. *Journal of Adolescent Research, 19*(1).

Byrnes & Ruby. (2007). *Comparing achievement between K–8 and middle schools: A large-scale empirical study.* Baltimore: Johns Hopkins University.

Gronna, S. (2006). Effects of grade school transition and school characteristics on eighth grade achievement. *PsychInfo*, University of Michigan database, 1999.

Howley, C. (1999). *The academic effectiveness of small-scale schooling* (ERIC ED No. 372897).

Howley, C. (2002). Grade span configurations. *The School Administrator* (Web edition, Ericdigest).

"K–8 comeback." (2008). *Duke Gifted Letter, 8*(1), Fall.

Moloney, J. (2008). American Association of School Administrators conference, as reported in Prescilla Pardini, *The School Administrator Newsletter,* 2002.

McEwin, K. (2004). *Program and practices in K–8 schools.* Westerville, OH: National Middle School Association.

Klump, J. (2006). What research says (or doesn't say) about K–8 versus middle school grade configurations. *Northwest Education, 11*(3). Retrieved February 22, 2009, from http://www.nwrel.org/nwedu/11-03/research/index.php

Offenberg, R. (2001, March). The efficacy of Philadelphia's K–8 schools compared to middle grade schools. *Middle School Journal.*

Simmons, R. G., & Blyth, D. A. (1987). *Moving into adolescence: The impact of pubertal change and school context.* New York: Aldine de Gruyter.

Wihry, D., Colordarci, T., & Meadows, C. (1992). Grade span and eighth grade academic achievement. *Journal of Research in Rural Education, 8*(2), 58–70.

Yakimowski, M. (2001). *Baltimore City Public School system: An examination of grade reconfiguration* (ERIC ED No. 1089674769).

Resource B

Content Standards Organizations

ARTS

The National Association of Music Educators: 1806 Robert Fulton Drive, Suite 1, Reston, VA, 20191. 703-860-4000. www.menc.org

CIVICS AND GOVERNMENT

Center for Civic Education: 5145 Douglas Fir Road, Calabasas, CA, 91302–1440. 818-591-9321. www.civiced.org

ECONOMICS

Council for Economic Education: 122 East 42nd Street, Suite 2600, New York, NY, 10168. 212-730-7007. www.nationalcouncil.org

ENGLISH LANGUAGE ARTS

National Council of Teachers of English: 1111 West Kenyon Road, Urbana, IL, 61801. 217-328-3870. www.ncte.org

International Reading Association: 800 Barksdale Road, PO Box 8139, Newark, DE, 19714–8139. 800-336-7323, ext. 266. www .reading.org

FOREIGN LANGUAGES

American Council on the Teaching of Foreign Languages: 1001 N. Fairfax Street, Suite 200, Alexandria, VA, 22314. 703-894-2900. www.actfl.org

GEOGRAPHY

National Council for Geographic Education: 1710 Sixteenth Street, NW, Washington, DC, 20009-3198. 202-360-4237. www.ncge.org

MATHEMATICS

National Council of Teachers of Mathematics: 1906 Association Drive, Reston, VA, 20191. 703-620-9840. www.nctm.org

PHYSICAL EDUCATION

National Association for Sport and Physical Education: 1900 Association Drive, Reston, VA, 20191. 703-476-3400. www.aahperd.org/Naspe/

SCIENCE

National Science Education Standards: National Academies Press, 500 Fifth Street, NW, Washington, DC, 20055. 888-624-8373. www.nap.edu

BENCHMARKS FOR SCIENCE LITERACY

American Association for the Advancement of Science: 1200 New York Avenue, NW, Washington, DC, 20005. 202–326–6400. www.aaas.org

SKILL STANDARDS (VOCATIONAL)

U.S. Department of Labor: 200 Constitution Avenue, NW, Washington, DC, 20210. 866-487-2365. www.dol.gov

U.S. Department of Education: Office of Vocational and Adult Education, 400 Maryland Avenue, SW, Washington, DC, 20202-7100. 1-800-872-5327. www.ed.gov/ovae

SOCIAL STUDIES

National Council for the Social Studies: 8555 16th Street, Suite 500, Silver Spring, MD, 20910. 1-301-588-1800. www.socialstudies.org

Resource C

Teaching Through the Internet

The Internet can serve as a major resource for K–8 teachers in meeting the needs of a wide range of students. Teachers can insert Internet sites into homework lessons, which in turn can be sent and returned on the computer. Below are found examples of Internet lessons using several common instructional designs:

CONTENT-BASED DESIGNS FOR KNOWLEDGE ACQUISITION

The Mayflower: Grades 1–3

The Pilgrims came to our country on ships such as the Mayflower. Let's visit some Internet sites to learn about this voyage.

What did the Mayflower look like? (http://www.nhusd.k12.ca.us/ALVE/wow/Molly/mayflower.html)

Who were the Mayflower passengers? (http://en.wikipedia.org/wiki/List_of_passengers_on_the_Mayflower)

Where did the Mayflower come ashore? (http://www.pilgrimhall.org/arrival.htm)

INQUIRY AND EXPLORATION LESSONS

Miss Shell Goes to Africa: Grade 4

"I have always wanted to travel to Africa," said Miss Shell. "It is such a big continent." (http://theafricachannel.com/aboutafrica.php)

"But I declare," she continued. "I want to see it from a car not a tour bus."
http://www.drivesouthafrica.co.za/experienceafrica/index.php?id=8)

"I am particularly interested in going to Tanzania," she exclaimed.
(http://images.google.com/images?q=Tanzania&hl=en&um=1&ie=UTF-
8&sa=X&oi=image_result_group&resnum=4&ct=title)

INTERDISCIPLINARY DESIGNS
FOR COMBINING KNOWLEDGE

Cultures of the World: Grades 5–8

Students can compare and contrast cultures by sharing different perspectives. In this lesson, different groups see a country by looking at the
following:

Factual data—(https://www.cia.gov/library/publications/the-world-
factbook/)

Geography—(http://www.nationalgeographic.com/maps)

Languages—(www.vistawide.com)

Religions—(http://www.mnsu.edu/emuseum/cultural/religion/)

Holidays—(http://www.worldbook.com/wb/Students?content_
spotlight/ holidays)

The objective is to be able to see the world through multiple lenses and
to compare and contrast differences in cultures.

COOPERATIVE LEARNING DESIGN:
COMBINING KNOWLEDGE

What is Pollution? Grades 5–6

Air pollution—(http://www.lbl.gov/Education/ELSI/pollution-main
.html)

Water pollution—(www.umich.edu/~gs265/society/waterpollution
.htm)

Noise Pollution—(http://www.infoplease.com/ce6/sci/A0835810.html)

Students will study independently or in small groups and then combine their findings (Jigsaw) to define pollution and its effects.

Resource D

Glossary

Ability grouping   Organizing pupils into homogeneous groups according to intellectual ability for instruction.

Accountability   Holding schools and teachers responsible for what students learn.

Accreditation   Recognition given to an educational institution that has met accepted standards applied to it by an outside agency.

Achievement test   Standardized test designed to measure how much has been learned from a particular subject.

Aligned   Term used to indicate that a school curriculum is matched with state and national standards as well as with state and national tests.

Balanced curriculum   A curriculum that incorporates all three areas: essential learning skills, subject content, and personal development.

Block scheduling   The reorganization of the daily or annual school schedule to allow students and teachers to have larger, more concentrated segments of time each day, week, or grading period on each subject. *See also* modular scheduling.

Career education   Instructional activities designed to provide students with the knowledge and skill necessary for selecting a vocation as well as for making decisions regarding educational and training options.

Certification   The licensure of personnel through prescribed programs of training and education.

Common planning time   A scheduling procedure that allows teachers to share the same period for instructional planning. The provision of common planning times facilitates collaborative efforts among teachers.

Competency   The demonstrated ability to perform specified acts at a particular level of skill or accuracy.

Competency-based instruction   Instructional programming that measures learning through the demonstration of predetermined outcomes. Mastery is assessed through an evaluation of the process as well as the product.

Cooperative learning   Two or more students working together on a learning task.

Core (fused) curriculum   Integration of two or more subjects; for example, English and social studies. Problem and theme orientations often serve as the integrating design. *See also* interdisciplinary program.

Criterion-referenced evaluation   Evaluation that measures success by the attainment of established levels of performance. Individual success is based wholly on the performance of the individual without regard to the performance of others.

Criterion-referenced test   Evaluation that measures performance compared with predetermined standards or objectives.

Cultural diversity   The existence of several different cultures within a group; encouraging each group to keep its individual qualities within the larger society.

Curriculum   The total experiences planned for a school or students.

Curriculum alignment   The matching of learning activities with desired outcomes, or matching what is taught to what is tested.

Curriculum compacting   Content development and delivery models that abbreviate the amount of time to cover a topic without compromising the depth and breadth of material taught.

Curriculum management planning   A systematic method of planning for change (Wiles–Bondi Curriculum Management Plan Model).

Departmentalization   The division of instructional staff, resources, and classes by academic disciplines; service delivery models such as separate general and special education programming; or some other arbitrary structure for compartmentalization.

Developmental tasks   Social, physical, maturational tasks regularly encountered by all individuals in our society as they progress from childhood to adolescence.

Early adolescence   The stage of human development generally between ages 10 and 14 when individuals begin to reach puberty.

Essential learning skills   Basic skills, such as reading, listening, and speaking, that are introduced in elementary school and reinforced in middle and high school.

Exploration   Regularly scheduled curriculum experiences designed to help students discover and examine learnings related to their changing needs, aptitudes, and interests. Often referred to as *the wheel* or *miniclasses.*

Flexible scheduling   Provisions in scheduling allowing for variance in length of time, order, or rotation of classes.

Formal operations   The last state in Piaget's theory of cognitive development, characterized by an ability to manipulate concepts abstractly and apply logical methods in the solution of complex problems. Children are not generally expected to exhibit these abilities before 11–15 years of age.

Global education   Instructional strategies and curriculum frameworks that include multiple, diverse, and international resources through the use of technology.

Graded school system   A division of schools into groups of students according to the curriculum or the ages of pupils, as in the six elementary grades.

Homogeneous grouping   Student grouping that divides learners on the basis of specific levels of ability, achievement, or interest. Sometimes referred to as *tracking*.

House plan   Type of organization in which the school is divided into units ("houses" or "learning communities"), with each having an identity and containing the various grades and, in large part, its own faculty. The purpose of a house plan is to achieve decentralization (closer student–faculty relationships) and easier and more flexible team-teaching arrangements.

Imitation   A process in which students learn by modeling the behavior of others.

Independent study   Work performed by students, without the direct supervision of the teacher, to develop self-study skills and to expand and deepen interests.

Individualized instruction   Instruction that focuses on the interests, needs, and achievements of individual learners.

Innovations   New instructional strategies, organizational designs, building rearrangements, equipment uses, or materials from which improved learning results are anticipated.

In-service education   Continuing education for teachers who are actually teaching, or who are in service (also called *staff development*).

Integration of disciplines   The organization of objectives under an interdisciplinary topic that allows students to use skills and knowledge from more than one content area within a given instructional activity or unit of study.

Interdisciplinary program   Instruction that integrates and combines subject matter ordinarily taught separately into a single organizational structure.

Interdisciplinary team   Combination of teachers from different subject areas who plan and conduct coordinated lessons in those areas for particular groups of pupils. Common planning time, flexible scheduling, and cooperation and communication among team teachers are essential to interdisciplinary teaming.

Metacognition   The process by which individuals examine their own thinking processes.

Middle school   A school between elementary and high school, housed separately, ideally in a building designed for its purpose, and covering usually three of the middle school years, beginning with Grade 5 or 6.

Minicourses   Special-interest (enrichment) activities of short duration that provide learning opportunities based on student interest, faculty expertise, and community involvement; also called *exploratory courses, short-interest-centered courses,* or *electives.*

Minimum competency testing   Exit-level tests designed to ascertain whether students have achieved basic levels of performance in such areas as reading, writing, and computation.

Mission statement   A statement of the goals or intent of a school.

Modular scheduling   The division of the school day into modules, typically 15 or 20 minutes long, with the number of modules used for various activities and experiences flexibly arranged.

Multicultural education   Educational goals and methods that teach students the value of cultural diversity.

Nongraded school   A type of school organization in which grade lines are eliminated for a sequence of 2 or more years.

Norm-referenced grading   Evaluation that measures a student's performance by comparing it with the performance of others.

Performance objective   Targeted outcome measures for evaluating the learning of particular process-based skills and knowledge.

Personal development   The intellectual, social, emotional, and moral growth of students fostered through such programs as advisor–advisee, developmental physical education, and minicourses.

Portfolio   A diversified combination of samples of a student's quantitative and qualitative work.

Progressive education   An educational philosophy emphasizing democracy, the importance of creative and meaningful activity, the real needs of students, and the relationship between school and community.

Readiness   The point at which a student is intellectually, physically, or socially able to learn a concept or exhibit a particular behavior.

Restructuring   The change of a school's entire program and procedure as opposed to the change of only one part of the curriculum.

Scope   The parameters of learning; for example, a subject-matter discipline sets its own scope, often by grade level.

Self-contained classroom   A form of classroom organization in which the same teacher conducts all or nearly all the instruction in all or most subjects in the same classroom for all or most of the school day.

Sequence   The organization of an area of study. Frequently, the organization is chronological, moving from simple to complex. Some sequences are spiraled, using structure, themes, or concept development as guidelines. A few schools use persistent life situations to shape sequence.

Special learning center   A designated area of a classroom, media center, or some other setting on the school campus with materials and activities designed to (a) enrich the existing educational program or (b) provide students with additional drill and practice in a targeted skill.

Staff development   A body of activities designed to improve the proficiencies of the educator–practitioner (sometimes called *in-service*).

Subject content   A type of curriculum that stresses the mastery of subject matter, with all other outcomes considered subsidiary. Also called *subject-matter curriculum grouping*.

Teachers Training Teachers (TTT)   An in-service process by which teachers receive instruction from peers, usually at the school level.

Team teaching   A plan by which several teachers, organized into a team with a leader, provide the instruction for a larger group of children than would usually be found in a self-contained classroom.

Tracking   The method of grouping students according to their ability level in homogeneous classes or learning experiences.

Unstructured time   Periods of time during the school day that have not been designated for a specific purpose and that present students with less supervision. The time between finishing lunch and the bell to return to the classroom is an example of unstructured time.

Work–study program   Collaborative efforts between the schools and community-based employers that allow students to earn course credit for time spent working. Students attend school for a designated number of periods per day and work a predetermined number of hours per week. Grades for work in the community are assigned based on the number of hours worked and the evaluation of the employer.

Resource E

Instructional Components for K–8 Education

MULTIPLE INTELLIGENCES

Pictorial explanation: http://pkab.files.wordpress.com/2008/07/multiple_intelligences_diagram3.jpg

Gardner's contribution to understanding: http://www.infed.org/thinkers/gardner.htm

LEARNING STYLES

An overview: http://www.funderstanding.com/content/learning-styles

Learning styles and multiple intelligence: http://www.ldpride.net/learningstyles .MI.htm

DIFFERENTIATED INSTRUCTION

Classroom implementation: http://www.frsd.k12.nj.us/rfmslibrarylab/di/differentiated_instruction.htm

For teachers' understanding: http://www.internet4classrooms.com/di.htm

COOPERATIVE LEARNING

Cooperative learning defined: http://edtech.kennesaw.edu/intech/cooperativelearning.htm

Research basis: http://www.teach-nology.com/currenttrends/cooperative _learning/slavin/

INTERDISCIPLINARY TEACHING

Definitions: http://www.sarasota.k12.fl.us/g2K/69.htm

Collaborative teaching examples: http://curriculalessons.suite101 .com/article.cfm/collaborative_teaching_exercises

PROBLEM-BASED LEARNING

Introduction and examples: http://www.udel.edu/pbl/

Teacher suggestions: http://www.cotf.edu/ete/teacher/teacherout.html

MENTORING

ABC's of school mentoring: http://gwired.gwu.edu/hamfish/merlin-cgi/ p/downloadFile/d/20696/n/off/other/1/name/abcspdf/

Role of the mentor: http://www.connecting-generations.org/creative-mentoring.html

SERVICE LEARNING

Definitions of service learning: http://www.newhorizons.org/strategies/ service_learning/front_service.htm

Projects: http://www.marylandpublicschools.org/MSDE/programs/ servicelearning/project_ideas

FLEXIBLE SCHEDULES

Research summary: http://www.nmsa.org/Research/Research Summaries/ FlexibleScheduling/tabid/1140/Default.aspx

Flexing in K–8 schools: http://www.osobear.com/FlexibleScheduling .html

LOOPING

A growing trend: http://www.post-gazette.com/regionstate/2000100 3100p3 .asp

Building teacher–student relationships: http://www.alliance.brown.edu/ pubs/ic/looping/looping.pdf

Resource F

Suggested Reading

Cherniss, C. (2000, April). *Emotional intelligence: What is it and why it matters.* Paper presented at Society of Industrial and Organizational Psychology, New Orleans.

Dauphinais, S. M., & Bradley, R. W. (1979). *IQ change and occupational level: A longitudinal study with Third Harvard Growth Study Participants.* (ERIC Document Reproduction Service No. EDEJ210637)

DesignShare. (2009). *DesignShare: Designing for the future of learning* [DesignShare home page]. Retrieved on February 27, 2009, from http://www.designshare.com/index.php/home

Gardner, H. (1983). *Frames of mind: The theory of multiple intelligence.* New York: Basic Books.

Pool, C. (1997). Up with emotional health. *Educational Leadership, 54*(8), 12–14.

Sternberg, R. (2005). The concept of intelligence and its role in lifelong learning and success. *American Psychologist, 52,* 1030–1037.

Tomlinson, C. (1999, October). *The challenge with mixed ability grouping.* Arlington, VA: American Association of School Administrators.

Tucker, T. (2000). Training tomorrow's leaders: Enhancing emotional intelligence. *Journal of Education for Business, 75*(6), 331–337.

Index

CORWIN
A SAGE Company

The Corwin logo—a raven striding across an open book—represents the union of courage and learning. Corwin is committed to improving education for all learners by publishing books and other professional development resources for those serving the field of PreK–12 education. By providing practical, hands-on materials, Corwin continues to carry out the promise of its motto: **"Helping Educators Do Their Work Better."**